THE PSYCHOLOGY OF BEAUTY

THE PSYCHOLOGY OF BEAUTY

BY

ETHEL D. PUFFER

BOSTON AND NEW YORK
HOUGHTON MIFFLIN COMPANY
The Riverside Press Cambridge

PREFACE

THE human being who thrills to the experience of beauty in nature and in art does not forever rest with that experience unquestioned. The day comes when he yearns to pierce the secret of his emotion, to discover what it is, and why, that has so stung him — to defend and to justify his transport to himself and to others. He seeks a reason for the faith that is in him. And so have arisen the speculative theories of the nature of beauty, on the one hand, and the studies of concrete beauty and our feelings about it, on the other. Speculative theory has taken its own way, however, as a part of philosophy, in relating the Beautiful to the other great concepts of the True and the Good; building up an architectonic of abstract ideas, far from the immediate facts and problems of the enjoyment of beauty. There has grown up, on the other hand, in the last years, a great literature of special studies in the facts of æsthetic production and enjoyment. Experiments with the æsthetic elements; investigations into the physiological psychology of æsthetic reactions; studies in the genesis and development of art forms, have multiplied apace. But these are still mere groups of facts for psychology; they have not been taken up into a single authoritative principle. Psychology cannot do justice to the imperative of beauty, by virtue of which, when we say " this is beautiful," we have a right to imply that the universe must agree with us. A synthesis of these tendencies in the study of beauty is needed, in which the results of modern psychology shall help to make intelligible a philosophical theory of beauty. The chief purpose of this book is to seek to effect such a union.

A way of defining Beauty which grounds it in general principles, while allowing it to reach the concrete case, is set forth in the essay on the Nature of Beauty. The following chapters aim to expand, to test, and to confirm this central theory, by showing, partly by the aid of the aforesaid special studies, how it accounts for our pleasure in pictures, music, and literature.

The whole field of beauty is thus brought under discussion; and therefore, though it nowhere seeks to be exhaustive in treatment, the book may fairly claim to be a more or less consistent and complete æsthetic theory, and hence to address itself to the student of æsthetics as well as to the general reader. The chapter on the Nature of Beauty, indeed, will doubtless be found by the latter somewhat technical, and should be omitted by all who definitely object to professional phraseology. The general conclusions of the book are sufficiently stated in the less abstract papers.

Of the essays which compose the following volume, the first, third, and last are reprinted, in more or less revised form, from the "Atlantic Monthly" and the "International Monthly." Although written as independent papers, it is thought that they do not unduly repeat each other, but that they serve to verify, in each of the several realms of beauty, the truth of the central theory of the book.

The various influences which have served to shape a work of this kind become evident in the reading; but I cannot refrain from a word of thanks to the teachers whose inspiration and encouragement first made it possible. I owe much gratitude to Professor Mary A. Jordan and Professor H. Norman Gardiner of Smith College, who in literature and in philosophy first set me in the way of æsthetic interest and inquiry, and to Professor Hugo Münsterberg of Harvard University, whose philosophical theories and scientific guidance have largely influenced my thought.

WELLESLEY COLLEGE, April 24, 1905.

CONTENTS

I

CRITICISM AND ÆSTHETICS

THE PSYCHOLOGY OF BEAUTY

I

CRITICISM AND ÆSTHETICS

IT is not so long ago that the field of literary criticism was divided into two opposing camps. France being the only country in the world where criticism is a serious matter, the battle waged most fiercely there, and doubtless greatly served to bring about the present general interest and understanding of the theoretical questions at issue. The combatants were, of course, the impressionistic and scientific schools of criticism, and particularly enlightening were the more or less recent controversies between MM. Anatole France and Jules Lemaître as representatives of the first, and M. Brunetière as the chief exponent of the second. They have planted their standards ; and we see that they stand for tendencies in the critical activity of every nation. The ideal of the impressionist is to bring a new piece of literature into being in some exquisitely happy characterization, — to create a lyric of criticism out of the unique pleasure of an æsthetic hour. The stronghold of the scientist, on the other hand, is the doctrine of literary evolution, and his aim is to show the history of literature as the history of a process, and the work of literature as a product; to explain it from its preceding causes, and to detect thereby the general laws of literary metamorphosis.

Such are the two great lines of modern criticism; their purposes and ideals stand diametrically opposed. Of late, however, there have not been wanting signs of a spirit of reconciliation, and of a tendency to concede the value, each in its own sphere, of different but complementary activities. Now and again the lion and the lamb have lain down together; one might almost say, on reading a delightful paper of Mr. Lewis E. Gates on Impressionism and Appreciation,[1] that the lamb had assimilated the lion. For the heir of all literary studies, according to Professor Gates, is the appreciative critic; and he it is who shall fulfill the true function of criticism. He is to consider the work of art in its historical setting and its psychological origin, " as a characteristic moment in the development of human spirit, and as a delicately transparent illustration of æsthetic law." But, " in regarding the work of art under all these aspects, his aim is, primarily, not to explain, and not to judge or dogmatize, but to enjoy; to realize the manifold charms the work of art has gathered unto itself from all sources, and to interpret this charm imaginatively to the men of his own day and generation."

Thus it would seem that if the report of his per-

[1] *Atlantic Monthly*, July, 1900.

sonal reactions to a work of literary art is the intention of the impressionist, and its explanation that of the scientist, the purpose of the appreciative critic is fairly named as the illuminating and interpreting reproduction of that work, from material furnished by those other forms of critical activity. Must, then, the method of appreciation, as combining and reconciling the two opposed views, forthwith claim our adherence? To put to use all the devices of science and all the treasures of scholarship for the single end of imaginative interpretation, for the sake of giving with the original melody all the harmonies of subtle association and profound meaning the ages have added, is, indeed, a great undertaking. But is it as valuable as it is vast? M. Brunetière has poured out his irony upon the critics who believe that their own reactions upon literature are anything to us in the presence of the works to which they have thrilled. May it not also be asked of the interpreter if his function is a necessary one? Do we require so much enlightenment, only to enjoy? Appreciative criticism is a salt to give the dull palate its full savor; but what literary epicure, what real book-lover, will acknowledge his own need of it? If the whole aim of appreciative criticism is to reproduce in other arrangement the contents, expressed and implied, and the emotional value, original and derived, of a piece of literature, the value of the end, at least to the intelligent reader, is out of all proportion to the laboriousness of the means. Sing, reading's a joy! For me, I read.

But a feeling of this kind is, after all, not a reason to be urged against the method. The real weakness of appreciative criticism lies elsewhere. It teaches us to enjoy; but are we to enjoy everything? Since its only aim is to reveal the "intricate implications" of a work of art; since it offers, and professes to offer, no literary judgments, — having indeed no explicit standard of literary value, — it must, at least on its own theory, take its objects of appreciation ready-made, so to speak, by popular acclaim. It possesses no criterion; it likes whate'er it looks on; and it can never tell us what we are not to like. That is unsatisfactory; and it is worse, — it is self-destructive. For, not being able to reject, appreciation cannot, in logic, choose the objects of its attention. But a method which cannot limit on its own principles the field within which it is to work is condemned from the beginning; it bears a fallacy at its core. In order to make criticism theoretically possible at all, the power to choose and reject, and so the pronouncing of judgment, must be an integral part of it.

To such a task the critic may lend himself without arousing our antagonism. We have no pressing need to know the latent possibilities of emotion for us in a book or a poem; but whether it is excellent or the reverse, whether "we were right in being moved by it," we are indeed willing to hear, for we desire to justify the faith that is in us.

If, then, the office of the judge be an essential part of the critical function, the appreciative critic, whatever his other merits, — and we shall examine them later, — fails at least of perfection. His scheme is not the ideal one ; and we may turn back, in our search for it, to a closer view of those which his was to supersede. Impressionism, however, is at once out of the running ; it has always vigorously repudiated the notion of the standard, and we know, therefore, that no more than appreciation can it choose its material and stand alone. But scientific criticism professes, at least, the true faith. M. Brunetière holds that his own method is the only one by which an impersonal and stable judgment can be rendered.

The doctrine of the evolution of literary species is more or less explained in naming it. Literary species, M. Brunetière maintains, do exist. They develop and are transformed into others in a way more or less analogous to the evolution of natural types. It remains to see on what basis an objective judgment can be given. Although M. Brunetière seems to make classification the disposal of a work in the hierarchy of species, and judgment the disposal of it in relation to others of its own species, he has never sharply distinguished between them ; so that we shall not be wrong in taking his three principles of classification, scientific, moral, and æsthetic, as three principles by which he estimates the excellence of a work. His own examples, in-

deed, prove that to him a thing is already judged
in being classified. The work of art is judged, then,
by its relation to the type. Is this position tenable?
I hold that, on the contrary, it precludes the possibility of a critical judgment; for the judgment of
anything always means judgment with reference to
the end for which it exists. A bad king is not the
less a bad king for being a good father; and if his
kingship is his essential function, he must be judged
with reference to that alone. Now a piece of literature is, with reference to its end, first of all a work
of art. It represents life and it enjoins morality,
but it is only as a work of art that it attains consideration; that, in the words of M. Lemaître, it
" exists " for us at all. Its aim is beauty, and beauty
is its excuse for being.

The type belongs to natural history. The one
principle at the basis of scientific criticism is, as
we have seen, the conception of literary history as
a process, and of the work of art as a product.
The work of art is, then, a moment in a necessary
succession, governed by laws of change and adaptation like those of natural evolution. But how can
the conception of values enter here? Excellence
can be attributed only to that which attains an
ideal end; and a necessary succession has no end
in itself. The " type," in this sense, is perfectly
hollow. To say that the modern chrysanthemum is
better than that of our forbears because it is more
chrysanthemum-like is true only if we make the

latter form the arbitrary standard of the chrysanthemum. If the horse of the Eocene age is inferior
to the horse of to-day, it is because, on M. Brunetière's principle, he is less horse-like. But who
shall decide which is more like a horse, the original
or the later development? No species which is constituted by its own history can be said to have an
end in itself, and can, therefore, have an excellence
to which it shall attain. In short, good and bad
can be applied to the moments in a necessary evolution only by imputing a fictitious superiority to
the last term; and so one type cannot logically be
preferred to another. As for the individual speci-
mens, since the conception of the type does not
admit the principle of excellence, conformity thereto
means nothing.

The work of art, on the other hand, as a thing
of beauty, is an attainment of an ideal, not a product, and, from this point of view, is related not
at all to the other terms of a succession, its causes
and its effects, but only to the abstract principles
of that beauty at which it aims. Strangely enough,
the whole principle of this contention has been admitted by M. Brunetière in a casual sentence, of
which he does not appear to recognize the full significance. "We acknowledge, of course," he says,
"that there is in criticism a certain difference from
natural history, since we cannot eliminate the subjective element if the capacity works of art have
of producing impressions on us makes a part of

their definition. It is not in order to be eaten that the tree produces its fruit." But this is giving away his whole position! As little as the conformity of the fruit to its species has to do with our pleasure in eating it, just so little has the conformity of a literary work to its *genre* to do with the quality by virtue of which it is defined as art.

The Greek temple is a product of Greek religion applied to geographical conditions. To comprehend it as a type, we must know that it was an adaptation of the open hilltop to the purpose of the worship of images of the gods. But the most penetrating study of the slow moulding of the type will never reveal how and why just those proportions were chosen which make the joy and the despair of all beholders. Early Italian art was purely ecclesiastical in its origin. The exigencies of adaptation to altars, convent walls, or cathedral domes explain the choice of subjects, the composition, even perhaps the color schemes (as of frescoes, for instance); and yet all that makes a Giotto greater than a Pictor Ignotus is quite unaccounted for by these considerations.

The quality of beauty is not evolved. All that comes under the category of material and practical purpose, of idea or of moral attitude, belongs to the succession, the evolution, the type. But the defining characters of the work of art are independent of time. The temple, the fresco, and the symphony, in the moment they become objects of the critical judgment, become also qualities of beauty and transparent examples of its laws.

If the true critical judgment, then, belongs to an order of ideas of which natural science can take no cognizance, the self-styled scientific criticism must show the strange paradox of ignoring the very qualities by virtue of which a given work has any value, or can come at all to be the object of æsthetic judgment. In two words, the world of beauty and the world of natural processes are incommensurable, and scientific criticism of literary art is a logical impossibility.

But the citadel of scientific criticism has yet one more stronghold. Granted that beauty, as an abstract quality, is timeless; granted that, in the judgment of a piece of literary art, the standard of value is the canon of beauty, not the type; yet the old order changeth. Primitive and civilized man, the Hottentot and the Laplander, the Oriental and the Slav, have desired differing beauties. May it, then, still be said that although a given embodiment of beauty is to be judged with reference to the idea of beauty alone, yet the concrete ideal of beauty must wear the manacles of space and time, — that the metamorphoses of taste preclude the notion of an objective beauty? And if this is true, are we not thrown back again on questions of genesis and development, and a study of the evolution, not of particular types of art, but of general æsthetic feeling; and, in consequence, upon a form of criticism which is scientific in the sense of being based on succession, and not on absolute value?

It is indeed true that the very possibility of a criticism which shall judge of æsthetic excellence must stand or fall with this other question of a beauty in itself, as an objective foundation for criticism. If there is an absolute beauty, it must be possible to work out a system of principles which shall embody its laws, — an æsthetic, in other words; and on the basis of that æsthetic to deliver a well-founded critical judgment. Is there, then, a beauty in itself? And if so, in what does it consist?

We can approach such an æsthetic canon in two ways: from the standpoint of philosophy, which develops the idea of beauty as a factor in the system of our absolute values, side by side with the ideas of truth and of morality, or from the standpoint of empirical science. For our present purpose, we may confine ourselves to the empirical facts of psychology and physiology.

When I feel the rhythm of poetry, or of perfect prose, which is, of course, in its own way, no less rhythmical, every sensation of sound sends through me a diffusive wave of nervous energy. I *am* the rhythm because I imitate it in myself. I march to noble music in all my veins, even though I may be sitting decorously by my own hearthstone; and when I sweep with my eyes the outlines of a great picture, the curve of a Greek vase, the arches of a cathedral, every line is lived over again in my own frame. And when rhythm and melody and forms and colors give me pleasure, it is because the imitating impulses and movements that have arisen in me are such as suit, help, heighten my physical organization in general and in particular. It may seem somewhat trivial to say that a curved line is pleasing because the eye is so hung as to move best in it; but we may take it as one instance of the numberless conditions for healthy action which a beautiful form fulfills. A well-composed picture calls up in the spectator just such a balanced relation of impulses of attention and incipient movements as suits an organism which is also balanced — bilateral — in its own impulses to movement, and at the same time stable; and it is the correspondence of the suggested impulses with the natural movement that makes the composition good. Besides the pleasure from the tone relations, — which doubtless can be eventually reduced to something of the same kind, — it is the balance of nervous and muscular tensions and relaxations, of yearnings and satisfactions, which are the subjective side of the beauty of a strain of music. The basis, in short, of any æsthetic experience — poetry, music, painting, and the rest — is beautiful through its harmony with the conditions offered by our senses, primarily of sight and hearing, and through the harmony of the suggestions and impulses it arouses with the whole organism.

But the sensuous beauty of art does not exhaust the æsthetic experience. What of the special emotions — the gayety or triumph, the sadness or peace or agitation — that hang about the work of art, and make, for many, the greater part of their delight in it? Those among these special emotions which belong to the subject-matter of a work — like our horror at the picture of an execution — need not here be discussed. To understand the rest we may venture for a moment into the realm of pure psychology. We are told by psychology that emotion is dependent on the organic excitations of any given idea. Thus fear at the sight of a bear is only the reverberation in consciousness of all nervous and vascular changes set up instinctively as a preparation for flight. Think away our bodily feelings, and we think away fear, too. And set up the bodily changes and the feeling of them, and we have the emotion that belongs to them even without the idea, as we may see in the unmotived panics that sometimes accompany certain heart disturbances. The same thing, on another level, is a familiar experience. A glass of wine makes merriment, simply by bringing about those organic states which are felt emotionally as cheerfulness. Now the application of all this to æsthetics is clear. All these tensions, relaxations, — bodily " imitations " of the form, — have each the emotional tone which belongs to it. And so if the music of a Strauss waltz makes us gay, and Hän-

del's Largo serious, it is not because we are reminded of the ballroom or of the cathedral, but
because the physical response to the stimulus of
the music is itself the basis of the emotion. What
makes the sense of peace in the atmosphere of the
Low Countries? Only the tendency, on following
those level lines of landscape, to assume ourselves
the horizontal, and the restfulness which belongs
to that posture. If the crimson of a picture by
Böcklin, or the golden glow of a Giorgione, or the
fantastic gleam of a Rembrandt speaks to me like
a human voice, it is not because it expresses to me
an idea, but because it impresses that sensibility
which is deeper than ideas, — the region of the
emotional response to color and to light. What is
the beauty of the " Ulalume," or " Kubla Khan," or
" Ueber allen Gipfeln " ? It is the way in which
the form in its exquisite fitness to our senses, and
the emotion belonging to that particular form as
organic reverberation therefrom, in its exquisite
fitness to thought, create in us a delight quite unaccounted for by the ideas which they express.
This is the essence of beauty, — the possession of
a quality which excites the human organism to
functioning harmonious with its own nature.

We can see in this definition the possibility of
an æsthetic which shall have objective validity because founded in the eternal properties of human
nature, while it yet allows us to understand that
in the limits within which, by education and envi-

ronment, the empirical man changes, his norms of beauty must vary, too. Ideas can change in interest and in value, but these energies lie much deeper than the idea, in the original constitution of mankind. They belong to the instinctive, involuntary part of our nature. They are changeless, just as the " eternal man " is changeless ; and as the basis of æsthetic feeling they can be gathered into a system of laws which shall be subject to no essential metamorphosis. So long as we laugh when we are joyful, and weep when we are sick and sorry ; so long as we flush with anger, or grow pale with fear, so long shall we thrill to a golden sunset, the cadence of an air, or the gloomy spaces of a cathedral.

The study of these forms of harmonious functioning of the human organism has its roots, of course, in the science of psychology, but comes, nevertheless, to a different flower, because of the grafting on of the element of æsthetic value. It is the study of the disinterested human pleasures, and, although as yet scarcely well begun, capable of a most detailed and definitive treatment.

This is not the character of those studies so casually alluded to by the author of " Impressionism and Appreciation," when he enjoins on the appreciative critic not to neglect the literature of æsthetics : " The characteristics of his [the artist's] temperament have been noted with the nicest loyalty ; and particularly the play of his special faculty, the im-

agination, as this faculty through the use of sensations and images and moods and ideas creates a
work of art, has been followed out with the utmost
delicacy of observation." But these are not properly studies in æsthetics at all. To find out what
is beautiful, and the reason for its being beautiful,
is the æsthetic task; to analyze the workings of
the poet's mind, as his conception grows and rami-
fies and brightens, is no part of it, because such a
study takes no account of the æsthetic value of the
process, but only of the process itself. The same
fallacy lurks here, indeed, as in the confusion of
the scientific critic between literary evolution and
poetic achievement, and the test of the fallacy is
this single fact: the psychological process in the
development of a dramatic idea, for instance, is,
and quite properly should be, from the point of
view of such analysis, exactly the same for a Shakespeare and for the Hoyt of our American farces.

The cause of the production of a work of art may
indeed be found by tracing back the stream of
thought; but the cause of its beauty is the desire
and the sense of beauty in the human heart. If a
given combination of lines and colors is beautiful,
then the anticipation of the combination as beautiful is what has brought about its incarnation. The
artist's attitude toward his vision of beauty, and the
art lover's toward that vision realized, are the same.
The only legitimate æsthetic analysis is, then, that
of the relation between the æsthetic object and the

lover of beauty, and all the studies in the psychology of invention — be it literary, scientific, or
practical invention — have no right to the other
name.

Æsthetics, then, is the science of beauty. It will
be developed as a system of laws expressing the
relation between the object and æsthetic pleasure in
it ; or as a system of conditions to which the object, in order to be beautiful, must conform. It is
hard to say where the task of the æsthetician ends,
and that of the critic begins ; and for the present,
at least, they must often be commingled. But they
are defined by their purposes : the end and aim of
one is a system of principles ; of the other, the
disposal of a given work with reference to those
principles ; and when the science of æsthetics shall
have taken shape, criticism will confine itself to
the analysis of the work into its æsthetic elements,
to the explanation (by means of the laws already
formulated) of its especial power in the realm of
beauty, and to the judgment of its comparative
æsthetic value.

The other forms of critical activity will then find
their true place as preliminaries or supplements to
the essential function of criticism. The study of
historical conditions, of authors' personal relations,
of the literary " moment," will be means to show
the work of art " as in itself it really is." Shall we
then say that the method of appreciation, being an
unusually exhaustive presentment of the object as

in itself it really is, is therefore an indispensable preparation for the critical judgment? The modern appreciator, after the model limned by Professor Gates, was to strive to get, as it were, the aerial perspective of a masterpiece, — to present it as it looks across the blue depths of the years. This is without doubt a fascinating study ; but it may be questioned if it does not darken the more important issue. For it is not the object as in itself it really is that we at last behold, but the object disguised in new and strange trappings. Such appreciation is to æsthetic criticism as the sentimental to the naïve poet in Schiller's famous antithesis. The virtue of the sentimental genius is to complete by the elements which it derives from itself an otherwise defective object. So the æsthetic critic takes his natural meed of beauty from the object; the appreciative critic seeks a further beauty outside of the object, in his own reflections and fancies about it. But if we care greatly for the associations of literature, we are in danger of disregarding its quality. A vast deal of pretty sentiment may hang about and all but transmute the most prosaic object. A sedan chair, an old screen, a sundial, — to quote only Austin Dobson, — need not be lovely in themselves to serve as pegs to hang a poem on ; and all the atmosphere of the eighteenth century may be wafted from a jar of potpourri. Read a lyric instead of a rose jar, and the rule holds as well. The man of feeling cannot but find all Ranelagh and Vauxhall in some icily regular effusion of the eighteenth century, and will take a deeper retrospective thrill from an old playbill than from the play itself. And since this is so, — since the interest in the overtones, the added value given by time, the value *for us*, is not necessarily related to the value as literature of the fundamental note, — to make the study of the overtones an essential part of criticism is to be guilty of the Pathetic Fallacy ; that is, the falsification of the object by the intrusion of ourselves, — the typical sentimental crime.

It seems to me, indeed, that instead of courting a sense for the aromatic in literature, the critic should rather guard himself against its insidious approaches. Disporting himself in such pleasures of the fancy, he finds it easy to believe, and to make us believe, that a piece of literature gains in intrinsic value from its power to stimulate his historical sense. The modern appreciative critic, in short, is too likely to be the dupe of his " sophisticated reverie," — like an epicure who should not taste the meat for the sauces. A master work, once beautiful according to the great and general laws, never becomes, properly speaking, either more or less so. If a piece of art can take us with its own beauty, there is no point in superimposing upon it shades of sentiment ; if it cannot so charm, all the rose-colored lights of this kind of appreciative criticism are unavailing.

The " literary " treatment of art, as the " emotional " treatment of literature, — for that is what " appreciation " and " interpretation " really are, — can completely justify itself only as the crowning touch of a detailed æsthetic analysis of those " orders of impression distinct in kind " which are the primary elements in our pleasure in the beautiful. It is the absence — and not only the absence, but the ignoring of the possibility — of such analysis which tempts one to rebel against such phrases as those of Professor Gates : " the splendid and victorious womanhood of Titian's Madonnas," " the gentle and terrestrial grace of motherhood in those of Andrea del Sarto," the " sweetly ordered comeliness of Van Dyck's." One is moved to ask if the only difference between a Madonna of Titian and one of Andrea is a difference of temper, and if the important matter for the critic of art is the moral conception rather than the visible beauty.

I cannot think of anything for which I would exchange the enchanting volumes of Walter Pater, and yet even he is not the ideal æsthetic critic whose duties he made clear. What he has done is to give us the most exquisite and delicate of interpretations. He has not failed to " disengage " the subtle and peculiar pleasure that each picture, each poem or personality, has in store for us ; but of analysis and explanation of this pleasure — of which he speaks in the Introduction to " The Renaissance " — there is no more. In the first lines of his paper on

Botticelli, the author asks, "What is the peculiar sensation which his work has the property of exciting in us?" And to what does he finally come? "The peculiar character of Botticelli is the result of a blending in him of a sympathy for humanity in its uncertain conditions . . . with his consciousness of the shadow upon it of the great things from which it sinks." But this is not æsthetic analysis! It is not even the record of a "peculiar sensation," but a complex intellectual interpretation. Where is the pleasure in the irrepressible outline, fascinating in its falseness, — in the strange color, like the taste of olives, of the Spring and the Pallas? So, also, his great passage on the Mona Lisa, his "Winckelmann," even his "Giorgione" itself, are merely wonderful delineations of the mood of response to the creations of the art in question. Such interpretation as we have from Pater is a priceless treasure, but it is none the less the final cornice, and not the corner stone of æsthetic criticism.

The tendency to interpretation without any basis in æsthetic explanation is especially seen in the subject of our original discussion, — literature. It is indeed remarkable how scanty is the space given in contemporary criticism to the study of an author's means to those results which we ourselves experience. Does no one really care how it is done? Or are they all in the secret, and interested only in the temperament expressed or the aspect of life envisaged in a given work? One would have thought that as the painter turned critic in Fromentin at least to a certain extent sought out and dealt with the hidden workings of his art, so the romancer or the poet-critic might also have told off for us " the very pulse of the machine." The last word has not been said on the mysteries of the writer's art. We know, it may be, how the links of Shakespeare's magic chain of words are forged, but the same cannot be said of any other poet. We have studied Dante's philosophy and his ideal of love; but have we found out the secrets of his " inventive handling of rhythmical language"? If Flaubert is universally acknowledged to have created a masterpiece in " Madame Bovary," should there not be an interest for criticism in following out, chapter by chapter, paragraph by paragraph, word by word, the meaning of what it is to be a masterpiece? But such seems not to be the case. Taine reconstructs the English temperament out of Fielding and Dickens; Matthew Arnold, although he deals more than others in first principles, never carries his analysis beyond the widest generalizations, like the requirement for " profound truth " and " high seriousness," for great poetry. And as we run the gamut of contemporary criticism, we find ever preoccupation with the personality of the writers and the ideas of their books. I recall only one example — the critical essays of Henry James — where the craftsman has dropped some hints on the ideals of the literary art; and even that, if I may be allowed the bull, in his novels rather than in his essays, for in critical theory he is the most ardent of impressionists. Whatever the cause, we cannot but allow the dearth of knowledge of, and interest in, the peculiar subject-matter of criticism, — the elements of beauty in a work of literature.

But although the present body of criticism consists rather of preliminaries and supplements to what should be its real accomplishment, these should not therefore receive the less regard. The impressionist has set himself a definite task, and he has succeeded. If not the true critic, he is an artist in his own right, and he has something to say to the world. The scientific critic has taken all knowledge for his province; and although we hold that it has rushed in upon and swamped his distinctly critical function, so long as we may call him by his other name of natural historian of literature, we can only acknowledge his great achievements. For the appreciative critic we have less sympathy as yet, but the " development of the luxurious intricacy and the manifold implications of our enjoyment " may fully crown the edifice of æsthetic explanation and appraisal of the art of every age. But all these, we feel, do not fulfill the essential function; the Idea of Criticism is not here. What the idea of criticism is we have tried to work out: a judgment of a work of art on the basis of the laws of beauty. That such laws there are, that they exist directly in the relation between the material form and the suggested physical reactions, and that they are practically changeless, even as the human instincts are changeless, we have sought to show. And if there can be a science of the beautiful, then an objective judgment on the basis of the laws of the beautiful can be rendered. The true end of criticism, therefore, is to tell us whence and why the charm of a work of art : to disengage, to explain, to measure, and to certify it. And this explanation of charm, and this stamping it with the seal of approval, is possible by the help, and only by the help, of the science of æsthetics, — a science now only in its beginning, but greatly to be desired in its full development.

How greatly to be desired we realize in divining that the present dearth of constructive and destructive criticism, of all, indeed, except interpretations and reports, is responsible for the modern mountains of machine-made literature. Will not the æsthetic critic be for us a new Hercules, to clear away the ever growing heap of formless things in book covers ? If he will teach us only what great art means in literature ; if he will give us never so little discussion of the first principles of beauty, and point the moral with some " selling books," he will at least have turned the flood. There are stories nowadays, but few novels, and plenty of spectacles, but no plays ; and how should we know the difference, never having heard what a novel ought to be ? But let the æsthetic critic give us a firm foundation for criticism, a real understanding of the conditions of literary art; let him teach us to know a novel or a play when we see it, and we shall not always mingle the wheat and the chaff.

II

THE NATURE OF BEAUTY

II

THE NATURE OF BEAUTY

EVERY introduction to the problems of æsthetics begins by acknowledging the existence and claims of two methods of attack, — the general, philosophical, deductive, which starts from a complete metaphysics and installs beauty in its place among the other great concepts; and the empirical, or inductive, which seeks to disengage a general principle of beauty from the objects of æsthetic experience and the facts of æsthetic enjoyment: Fechner's "æsthetics from above and from below."

The first was the method of æsthetics *par excellence.* It was indeed only through the desire of an eighteenth-century philosopher, Baumgarten, to round out his "architectonic" of metaphysics that the science received its name, as designating the theory of knowledge in the form of feeling, parallel to that of "clear," logical thought. Kant, Schelling, and Hegel, again, made use of the concept of the Beautiful as a kind of keystone or cornice for their respective philosophical edifices. Æsthetics, then, came into being as the philosophy of the Beautiful, and it may be asked why this philosophical æsthetics does not suffice — why beauty should need for its understanding also an æsthetics " von unten."

The answer is not that no system of philosophy is universally accepted, but that the general æsthetic theories have not, as yet at least, succeeded in answering the plain questions of " the plain man " in regard to concrete beauty. Kant, indeed, frankly denied that the explanation of concrete beauty, or " Doctrine of Taste," as he called it, was possible, while the various definers of beauty as " the union of the Real and the Ideal," " the expression of the Ideal to Sense," have done no more than he. No one of these æsthetic systems, in spite of volumes of so-called application of their principles to works of art, has been able to furnish a criterion of beauty. The criticism of the generations is summed up in the mild remark of Fechner, in his " Vorschule der Aesthetik," to the effect that the philosophical path leaves one in conceptions that, by reason of their generality, do not well fit the particular cases. And so it was that empirical aesthetics arose, which does seek to answer those plain questions as to the enjoyment of concrete beauty down to its simplest forms, to which philosophical æsthetics had been inadequate.

But it is clear that neither has empirical æsthetics said the last word concerning beauty. Criticism is still in a chaotic state that would be impossible if æsthetic theory were firmly grounded.

This situation appears to me to be due to the inherent inadequacy and inconclusiveness of empirical æsthetics when it stands alone; the grounds of this inadequacy I shall seek to establish in the following.

Granting that the aim of every æsthetics is to determine the Nature of Beauty, and to explain our feelings about it, we may say that the empirical treatments propose to do this either by describing the æsthetic object and extracting the essential elements of Beauty, or by describing the æsthetic experience and extracting the essential elements of æsthetic feeling, thereby indicating the elements of Beauty as those which effect this feeling.

Now the bare description and analysis of beautiful objects cannot, logically, yield any result; for the selection of cases would have to be arbitrary, and would be at the mercy of any objection. To any one who should say, But this is not beautiful, and should not be included in your inventory, answer could be made only by showing that it had such and such qualities, the very, by hypothesis, unknown qualities that were to be sought. Moreover, the field of beauty contains so many and so heterogeneous objects, that the retreat to their only common ground, æsthetic feeling, appears inevitable. A statue and a symphony can be reduced to a common denominator most easily if the states of mind which they induce are compared. Thus the analysis of objects passes naturally over to the analysis of mental states — the point of view of psychology.

There is, however, a method subsidiary to the preceding, which seeks the elements of Beauty in a study of the genesis and the development of art forms. But this leaves the essential phenomenon absolutely untouched. The general types of æsthetic expression may indeed have been shaped by social forces, — religious, commercial, domestic, — but as social products, not as æsthetic phenomena. Such studies reveal to us, as it were, the excuse for the fact of music, poetry, painting — but they tell us nothing of the reason why beautiful rather than ugly forms were chosen, as who should show that the bird sings to attract its mate, ignoring the relation and sequence of the notes. The decorative art of most savage tribes, for instance, is nearly all of totemic origin, and the decayed and degraded forms of snake, bird, bear, fish, may be traced in the most apparently empty geometric patterns ; — but what does this discovery tell us of the essentially decorative quality of such patterns or of the nature of beauty in form ? The study of the Gothic cathedral reveals the source of its general plan and of its whole scheme of ornament in detailed religious symbolism. Yet a complete knowledge of the character of the religious feeling which impelled to this monumental expression, and of the genesis of every element of structure, fails to account for the essential beauty of rhythm and proportion in the finished work. These researches, in short, explain the reason for the existence, but not for the quality, of works of art.

Thus it is in psychology that empirical æsthetics finds its last resort. And indeed, our plain man might say, the æsthetic experience itself is inescapable and undeniable. You know that the sight or the hearing of this thing gives you a thrill of pleasure. You may not be able to defend the beauty of the object, but the fact of the experience you have. The psychologist, seeking to analyze the vivid and unmistakable æsthetic experience, would therefore proceed somewhat as follows. He would select the salient characteristics of his mental state in presence of a given work of art. He would then study, by experiment and introspection, how the particular sense-stimulations of the work of art in question could become the psychological conditions of these salient characteristics. Thus, supposing the æsthetic experience to have been described as " the conscious happiness in which one is absorbed, and, as it were, immersed in the sense-object," [1] the further special aim, in connection with a picture, for instance, would be to show how the sensations and associated ideas from color, line, composition, and all the other elements of a picture may, on general psychological principles, bring about this state of happy absorption. Such elements as can be shown to have a direct relation to the

[1] M. W. Calkins: *An Introduction to Psychology*, 1902, p. 278.

æsthetic experience are then counted as elements of the beauty of the æsthetic object, and such as are invariable in all art forms would belong to the general formula or concept of Beauty.

This, it seems to me, is as favorable a way as possible of stating the possibilities of an independent æsthetic psychology.

Yet this method, as it works out, does not exhaust the problem the solution of which was affirmed to be the aim of every æsthetics. The æsthetic experience is very complex, and the theoretical consequences of emphasizing this or that element very great. Thus, if it were held that the characteristics of the æsthetic experience could be given by the complete analysis of a single well-marked case, — say, our impressions before a Doric column, or the Cathedral of Chartres, or the Giorgione Venus, — it could be objected that for such a psychological experience the essential elements are hard to isolate. The cathedral is stone rather than staff; it is three hundred rather than fifty feet high. Our reaction upon these facts may or may not be essentials to the æsthetic moment, and we can know whether they are essentials only by comparison and exclusion. It might be said, therefore, that the analysis of a single, though typical, æsthetic experience is insufficient; a wide induction is necessary. Based on the experience of many people, in face of the same object? But to many there would be no æsthetic experience. On that of one person, over an extensive field of objects? How, then, determine the limits of this field? Half of the dispute of modern æsthetics is over the right to include in the material for this induction various kinds of enjoyment which are vivid, not directly utilitarian, but traditionally excluded from the field. Guyau, for instance, in a charming passage of his " Problèmes de l'Esthétique Contemporaine," argues for the æsthetic quality of the moment when, exhausted by a long mountain tramp, he quaffed, among the slopes of the Pyrenees, a bowl of foaming milk. The same dispute appears, in more complicated form, in the conflicting dicta of the critics.

If we do not know what part of our feeling is æsthetic feeling, how can we go farther? If the introspecting subject cannot say, *This* is æsthetic feeling, it is logically impossible to make his state of mind the basis for further advance. It is clear that the great question is of what one has a right to include in the æsthetic experience. But that one should have such a " right " implies that there is an imperative element in the situation, an absolute standard somewhere.

It seems to me that the secret of the difficulty lies in the nature of the situation, with which an empirical treatment must necessarily fail to deal. What we have called " the æsthetic experience " is really a positive toning of the general æsthetic attitude. This positive toning corresponds to æsthetic excellence in the object. But wherever the concept of excellence enters, there is always the implication of a standard, value, judgment. But where there is a standard there is always an implicit *a priori*, — a philosophical foundation.

If, then, a philosophical method is the last resort and the first condition of a true æsthetics, what is the secret of its failure? For that it has failed seems to be still the consensus of opinion. Simply, I believe and maintain, the unreasonable and illogical demand which, for instance, Fechner makes in the words I have quoted, for just this *immediate* application of a philosophical definition to concrete cases. Who but an Hegelian philosopher, cries Professor James, ever pretended that reason in action was *per se* a sufficient explanation of the political changes in Europe? Who but an Hegelian philosopher, he might add, ever pretended that " the expression of the Idea to Sense " was a sufficient explanation of the Sistine Madonna? But I think the Hegelian — or other — philosopher might answer that he had no need so to pretend. Such a philosophical definition, as I hope to show, cannot possibly apply to particular cases, and should not be expected to do so.

Beauty is an excellence, a standard, a value. But value is in its nature teleological; is of the nature of purpose. Anything has value because it fulfills an end, because it is good for something in the world. A thing is not beautiful because it has value, — other things have that, — it has value because it is beautiful, because it fulfills the end of Beauty. Thus the metaphysical definition of Beauty must set forth what this end of Beauty is, — what it serves in the universe.

But to determine what anything does, or fulfills, or exemplifies, is not the same as to determine what it is in itself. The most that can be said is that the end, or function, shapes the means or constitution. The end is a logical imperative. Beauty does, and must do, such things. To ask *how*, is at once to indicate an ultimate departure from the philosophical point of view; for the means to an end are different, and to be empirically determined.

Now the constitution of Beauty can be only the means to the end of Beauty, — that combination of qualities in the object which will bring about the end fixed by philosophical definition. The end is general; the means may be of different kinds. Evidently, then, the philosophical definition cannot be applied directly to the object until the possibilities, conditions, and limitations of that object's fitness for the purpose assigned are known. We cannot ask, Does the Sistine Madonna express the Idea to Sense? until we know all possibilities and conditions of the visual for attaining that expression. But, indeed, the consideration of causes and effects suggests at once that natural science must guide further investigation. Philosophy must lay down what Beauty has to do; but since it is in our *experience* of Beauty that its end is accomplished, since the analysis of such experience and the study of its contributing elements is a work of the natural science of such experience — it would follow that psychology must deal with the various means through which this end is to be reached.

Thus we see that Fechner's reproach is unjustified. Those concepts which are too general to apply to particular cases are not meant to do so. If a general concept expresses, as it should, the place of Beauty in the hierarchy of metaphysical values, it is for the psychologist of æsthetics to develop the means by which that end can be reached in the various realms in which works of art are found.

Nor can we agree with Santayana's dictum [1] that philosophical æsthetics confuses the import of an experience with the explanation of its cause. It need not. The æsthetic experience is indeed caused by the beautiful object, but the beautiful object itself is caused by the possibility of the æsthetic experience, — *beauty as an end* under the conditions of human perception. Thus the Nature of Beauty is related to its import, or meaning, or end, as means to that end; and therefore the import of an experience may well point out to us the constitution of the cause of that experience. A work of art, a piece of nature, is judged by its degree of attainment to that end; the *explanation* of its beauty — of its degree of attainment, that is — is

[1] *The Sense of Beauty*, 1898. Intro.

found in the effect of its elements, according to psychological laws, on the æsthetic subject.

Such a psychological study of the means by which the end of Beauty is attained is the only method by which we can come to an explanation of the wealth of concrete beauty. The concept of explanation, indeed, is valid only within the realm of causes and effects. The aim of æsthetics being conceded, as above, to be the determination of the Nature of Beauty and the explanation of our feelings about it, it is evident at this point that the Nature of Beauty must be determined by philosophy; but the general definition having been fixed, the meaning of the work of art having been made clear, the only possible explanation of our feelings about it — the æsthetic experience, in other words — must be gained from psychology. This method is not open to the logical objections against the preceding. No longer need we ask what has a right to be included in the æsthetic experience. That has been fixed by the definition of Beauty. But how the beautiful object brings about the æsthetic experience, the boundaries of which are already known, is clearly matter for psychology.

The first step must then be to win the philosophical definition of Beauty. It was Kant, says Hegel, who spoke the first rational word concerning Beauty. The study of his successors will reveal, I believe, that the æsthetic of the great system of idealism forms, on the whole, one identical doctrine.

It is worth while to dwell somewhat on this point, because the traditional view of the relation of the æsthetic of Kant, Schiller, Schelling, and Hegel is otherwise. Kant's starting-point was the discovery of the normative, " over-individual " nature of Beauty, which we have just found to be the secret of the contradictions of empirical æsthetics. Yet he came to it at the bidding of quite other motives.

Kant's æsthetics was meant to serve as the keystone of the arch between sense and reason. The discovery of all that is implicit in the experience of the senses had led him to deny the possibility of knowledge beyond the matter of this experience. Yet the reason has an inevitable tendency to press beyond this limit, to seek all-embracing, absolute unities, — to conceive an unconditioned totality. Thus the reason presents us with the ideas — beyond all possibility of knowledge — of the Soul, the World, and God. In the words of Kant, the Ideas of Reason lead the understanding to the consideration of Nature according to a principle of completeness, although it can never attain to this. Can there be a bridge across this abyss between sense and reason ? then asks Kant ; which bridge he believes himself to have found in the æsthetic faculty. For on inquiring what is involved in the judgment, " This is beautiful," he discovers that such a judgment is " universal " and " necessary," inasmuch as it implies that every normal spectator must acknowledge its validity, that it is "disinterested" because it rests on the "appearance of the object without demanding its actual existence," and that it is "immediate" or "free," as it acknowledges the object as beautiful without definite purpose, as of adaptation to use. But how does this judgment constitute the desired bond between sense and reason? Simply in that, though applied to an object of the senses, it has yet all the marks of the Idea of Reason, — it is universal, necessary, free, unconditioned; it has "the principle of completeness." And as for the object itself, it is judged *as if it were* perfect, and so fulfills those demands of reason which elsewhere in the world of sense are unsatisfied.

The two important factors, then, of Kant's æsthetics are its reconciliation of sense and reason in beauty, and its reference of the "purposiveness" of beauty to the cognitive faculty.

Schiller has been given the credit of transcending Kant's "subjective" æsthetic through his emphasis on the significance of the beautiful object. It is not bound by a conception to which it must attain, so that it is perceived as if it were free. Nor do we desire the reality of it to use for ourselves or for others; so that we are free in relation to it. It, the object, is thus "the vindication of freedom in the world of phenomena," that world which is otherwise a binding necessity. But it would seem that this had been already taught by Kant

himself, and that Schiller has but enlivened the
subject by his two illuminating phrases, " æsthetic
semblance " and the " play-impulse," to denote
the real object of the æsthetic desire and the true
nature of that desire; form instead of material
existence, and a free attitude instead of serious
purpose. Still, his insistence on Beauty as the realization of freedom may be said to have paved
the way for Schelling's theory, in which the æsthetic reaches its maximum of importance.

The central thought of the Absolute Idealism of
Schelling is the underlying identity of Nature and
the Self. In Nature, from matter up to the organism, the objective factor predominates, or, in Schelling's phrase, the conscious self is determined by
the unconscious. In morality, science, the subjective factor predominates, or the unconscious is determined by the conscious. But the work of art is
a natural appearance and so unconscious, and is
yet the product of a conscious activity. It gives,
then, the equilibrium of the real and ideal factors,
— just that repose of reconciliation or " indifference " which alone can show the Absolute. But —
and this is of immense importance for our theory
— in order to explain the identity of subject and
object, the Ego must have an intuition, through
which, in one and the same appearance, it is *in itself* at once conscious and unconscious, and this
condition is given in the æsthetic experience. The
beautiful is thus the solution of the riddle of the

universe, for it is the possibility of the explicit consciousness of the unity of Nature and the Self — or the Absolute.

So Beauty is again the pivot on which a system turns. Its place is not essentially different from that which it held in the systems of Kant and Schiller. As the objective possibility for the bridge between sense and reason, as the vindication of freedom in the phenomenal world, and as the vindication of the possible unity of the real and the ideal, or nature and self, the world-elements, its philosophical significance is nearly the same.

With Hegel Beauty loses little of its commanding position. The universe is in its nature rational ; Thought and Being are one. The world-process is a logical process ; and nature and history, in which spirit of the world realizes itself, are but applied logic. The completely fulfilled or expressed Truth is then the concrete world-system ; at the same time the life or self of the universe ; the Absolute. This Hegel calls the Idea, and he defines Beauty as the expression of the Idea to sense.

This definition would seem to be as to the letter in accord with the general tendency we have already outlined. It might be said that it is but another phrasing of Schelling's thought of the Absolute as presented to the Ego in Beauty. But not so. For Schelling, the æsthetic is a schema or form, — that is, the form of balance, equilibrium, reconciliation of the rational ideal, — not a content. But Hegel's

Beauty *expresses* the Idea by the way of information or association. That this is true any one of his traditional examples makes evident. Correggio's Madonna of the St. Sebastian is found by him inferior to the Sistine Madonna. Why? " In the first picture we have the dearest and loveliest of human relations consecrated by contrast with what is Divine. In the second picture we have the Divine relation itself, showing itself under the limitations of the human." [1] Dutch painting, he tells us, ought not to be despised; " for it is this fresh and wakeful freedom and vitality of mind in apprehension and presentation that forms the highest aspect of these pictures." And a commentator adds, " The spontaneous joy of the perfect life is figured to this lower sphere." His whole treatment of Art as a symbol confirms this view, as do all his criticisms. Art or Beauty shall reveal to our understanding the eternal Ideal.

On comparing this with what we have won from Kant, Schiller, and Schelling, the divergence becomes apparent. I have tried to show that there is no essential difference between these three either in their general view of the æsthetic experience, or in the degree of objectivity of their doctrine of Beauty. They do not contradict one another. They merely emphasize now the unity, now the reconciliation of opposites, in the æsthetic experience. The experience of the beautiful constitutes a reconciliation of

[1] Kedney's Hegel's *Æsthetics*, 1892, p. 158.

the warring elements of experience, in a world in which the demands of Reason seem to conflict with the logic of events, and the beautiful object is such that it constitutes the permanent possibility for this reconciliation.

But the attempt to include Hegel within this circle reveals at once the need of further delimitation. The beautiful is to reveal, and to vindicate in revealing, the union of the world-elements, that is, the spirit of the world. On Hegel's own principles, the Idea should be " expressed to sense." Now if this expression is not, after all, directly to sense, but the sense gives merely the occasion for passing over to the thought of the Divine, it would seem that the Beauty is not after all in the work of art, but out of it. The Infinite, or the Idea, or the fusion of real and ideal, must be *shown* to sense.

Is there any way in which this is conceivable? We cannot completely express to sense Niagara Falls or the Jungfrau, for they are infinitely beyond the possibilities of imitation. Yet the particular contour of the Jungfrau is never mistaken in the smallest picture. In making a model of Niagara we should have to reproduce the relation between body of water, width of stream, and height of fall, and we might succeed in getting the peculiar effect of voluminousness which marks that wonder of Nature. The soaring of a lark is not like the pointing upward of a slender Gothic spire, yet there is a likeness in the attitudes with

which we follow them.   All these cases have certain
form-qualities in common, by virtue of which they
resemble each other.   Now it is these very form-
qualities which Kant is using when he takes the
æsthetic judgment as representative of reason in
the world of sense because it *shows the qualities*
of the ideas of reason, — that is, unconditional totality or freedom.   And we might, indeed, hope to
" express the Idea to sense " if we could find for
it a form-quality, or subjectively, in the phrase of
Kant, a *form of reflection*.

What is the form of reflection for the Absolute,
the Idea?   It would appear to be a combination of
Unity and Totality — self-completeness.   An object,
then, which should be self-complete from all possible
points of view, to which could be applied the "form
of reflection" for the Absolute, would, therefore,
alone truly express it, and so alone fulfill the end of
Beauty.   The Idea would be *there* in its *form;* it
would be shown to sense, and so first fully expressed.

With this important modification of Hegel's definition of Beauty, which brings it into line with the
point of view already won, I believe the way is
at last opened from the traditional philosophy of
æsthetics to a healthy and concrete psychological
theory.

But must every self-complete object give rise to
the æsthetic experience?   An object is absolutely
self-complete only for the perceiving subject; it is
so, in other words, only when it produces a self-com-

plete experience for that subject. If reconciliation
of the warring elements of the universe is the end
of Beauty it must take place not *for*, but *in*, the
human personality ; it must not be understood, but
immediately, completely experienced ; it should be
such that the Unity of the World should be realized in the subject of the æsthetic experience,
the lover of beauty. The beautiful object would
be not that which should show in outline form,
or remind of, this Unity of the World, but which
should create for the subject the moment of self-
completeness ; which should inform the æsthetic
subject with that unity and self-completeness which
are the " forms of reflection " of the Infinite.
The subject should be not a mirror of perfection,
but a state of perfection. Only in this sense does
the concept of reconciliation come to its full meaning. Not because I see freedom, but because I am
free ; not because I think of God, or the Infinite, or
the one, but because I am for the moment complete,
at the highest point of energy and unity, does the
æsthetic experience constitute such a reconciliation.
Not because I behold the Infinite, but because
I have, myself, a moment of perfection. Herein
it is that our theory constitutes a complete contradiction to all " expression " or " significance "
theories of the Beautiful, and does away with the
necessity those theories are under of reading sermons into stones. The yellow primrose needs not
to remind us of the harmony of the universe, or

to have any ulterior significance whatever, if it gives by its own direct simple stimulation a moment of Unity and Self-completeness. That immediate experience indeed contains in itself the " form of reflection" of the Absolute, and it is through this that we so often pass, in the enjoyment of Beauty, to the thought of the divine. But that thought is a corollary, a secondary effect, not an essential part of the æsthetic moment. There is a wonderful bit of unconscious æsthetics in the following passage from Sénancour, touching the " secret of relation " we have just analyzed.

" It was dark and rather cold. I was gloomy, and walked because I had nothing to do. I passed by some flowers placed breast-high upon a wall. A jonquil in bloom was there. It is the strongest expression of desire : it was the first perfume of the year. I felt all the happiness destined for man. This unutterable harmony of souls, the phantom of the ideal world, arose in me complete. I never felt anything so great or so instantaneous. I know not what shape, what analogy, what secret of relation it was that made me see in this flower a limitless beauty. . . . I shall never inclose in a conception this power, this immensity that nothing will express ; this form that nothing will contain ; this ideal of a better world which one feels, but which it would seem that nature has not made." [1]

[1] Translation by Carleton Noyes : *The Enjoyment of Art*, 1903, p. 65.

Our philosophical definition of Beauty has thus taken final shape. The beautiful object possesses those qualities which bring the personality into a state of unity and self-completeness. Lightly to cast aside such a definition as abstract, vague, empty, is no less short sighted than to treat the idea of the Absolute Will, of the Transcendental Reason, of the Eternal Love, as mere intellectual factors in the æsthetic experience. It should not be criticised as giving " no objective account of the nature and origin of Beauty." The nature of Beauty is indicated in the definition ; the origin of Beauty may be studied in its historical development ; its reason for being is simply the desire of the human heart for the perfect moment.

Beauty is to bring unity and self-completeness into the personality. By what means ? What causes can bring about this effect? When we enter the realm of causes and effects, however, we have already left the ground of philosophy, and it is fitting that the concepts which we have to use should be adapted to the empirical point of view. The personality, as dealt with in psychology, is but the pyschophysical organism ; and we need to know only how to translate unity and self-completeness into psychological terms.

The psychophysical organism is in a state of unity either when it is in a state of virtual congealment or emptiness, as in a trance or ecstasy ; or when it is in a state of repose, without tendency to change.

Secondly, the organism is self-complete when it is at the highest possible point of tone, of functional efficiency, of enhanced life. Then a combination of favorable stimulation and repose would characterize the æsthetic feeling.

But it may be said that stimulation and repose are contradictory concepts, and we must indeed admit that the absolute repose of the hypnotic trance is not æsthetic, because empty of stimulus. The only æsthetic repose is that in which stimulation resulting in impulse to movement or action is checked or compensated for by its antagonistic impulse ; inhibition of action, or action returning upon itself, combined with heightening of tone. But this is *tension, equilibrium,* or *balance of forces*, which is thus seen to be *a general condition of all æsthetic experience*. The concept is familiar in pictorial composition and to some extent also in music and poetry, but here first appears as grounded in the very demand for the union of repose with activity.

Moreover, this requirement, which we have derived from the logical concepts of unity and totality, as translated into psychological terms, receives confirmation from the nature of organic life. It was the perfect moment that we sought, and we found it in the immediate experience of unity and self-completeness ; and unity for a living being *can* only be equilibrium. Now it appears that an authoritative definition of the general nature of an organism makes it " so built, whether on mechanical principles or not, that every deviation from the equilibrium point sets up a tendency to return to it." [1] Equilibrium, in greater or less excursions from the centre, is thus the ultimate nature of organic life. The perfect equilibrium, that is, equilibrium with heightened tone, will then give the perfect moment.

The further steps of æsthetics are then toward analysis of the psychological effect of all the elements which enter into a work of art, with reference to their effect in producing stimulation or repose. What colors, forms, tones, emotions, ideas, favorably stimulate? What combinations of these bring to repose? All the modern studies in so-called physiological æsthetics, into the emotional and other — especially motor — effects of color, tone-sensation, melodic sequence, simple forms, etc., find here their proper place.

A further important question, as to the fitting psychological designation of the æsthetic state, is now suggested. Some authorities speak of the æsthetic attitude or activity, describing it as " sympathetic imitation" or "absorption;" others of the æsthetic pleasure. But, according to our definition of the æsthetic experience as a combination of favorable stimulation with repose, this state, as involving "a distinctive feeling-tone and a characteristic trend of activity aroused by a certain situation," [2] can be no other than an emotion. This view is

[1] L. T. Hobhouse, *Mind in Evolution.*
[2] Baldwin's *Dict. of Phil. and Psychol.* Art. " Emotion."

confirmed by introspection; we speak of æsthetic
activity and æsthetic pleasure, but we are conscious
of a complete arrest, and sometimes of a very distinct divergence from pure pleasure. The experience is unique, it seems to defy description, to be
intense, vivid, and yet — like itself alone. Any
attempt to disengage special, already known emotions, even at the play or in hearing music, is often
in vain, in just those moments when our excitement
is most intense. But the hypothesis of a unique
emotion, parallel to those of joy, fear, etc., and with
a psychological basis as outlined, would account for
these facts. The positive toning of the experience
— what we call æsthetic pleasure — is due not only
to the favorable stimulation, but also to the fact
that the very antagonism of impulses which constitutes repose heightens tone while it inhibits action.
Thus the conditions of both factors of æsthetic
emotion tend to induce pleasure.

It is, then, clear that no specific æsthetic pleasure
need be sought. The very phrase, indeed, is a mis-
nomer, since all pleasure is qualitatively the same,
and differentiated only by the specific activities
which it accompanies. It is also to be noted that
those writers on æsthetics who have dwelt most on
æsthetic pleasure have come in conclusion only to
specific activities, like the "imitation" of Groos, for
instance. In the light of the just-won definition
of æsthetic emotion, it is interesting to examine
some of the well-known modern æsthetic theories.

Lipps defines the æsthetic experience as a "thrill of sympathetic feeling," Groos as "sympathetic imitation," evidently assuming that pleasure accompanies this. But there are many feelings of sympathy, and joyful ones, which do not belong to the æsthetic realm. In the same way, not all "imitation" is accompanied by pleasure, and not all of that falls within the generally accepted æsthetic field. If these definitions were accepted as they stand, all our rejoicings with friends, all our inspiration from a healthy, magnetic presence must be included in it. It is clear that further limitation is necessary; but if to this sympathetic imitation, this living through in sympathy, we add the demand for repose, the necessary limitation is made. Physical exercise in general, or the instinctive imitation of energetic, or easy (in general *favorable*) movements, is pleasurable, indeed, but the experience is not æsthetic, — as is quite clear, indeed, to common sense, — and it is not æsthetic because it is the contradiction of repose. A particular case of the transformation of pleasurable physical exercise into an æsthetic activity is seen in the experience of symmetrical or balanced form; any moderate, smooth exercise of the eye is pleasurable, but this alone induces a state of the whole organism combining repose with stimulation.

The theories of Külpe and Santayana, while they definitely mark out the ground, seem to me in need of addition. "Absorption in the object in respect to its bare quality and conformation " does not, of course, give the needed information, for objective beauty, of the character of this conformation or form. But yet, it might be said that the content of beauty might conceivably be deduced from the psychological conditions of absorption. In the same way, Santayana's "Beauty as objectified pleasure," or pleasure as the quality of a thing, is neither a determination of objective beauty nor a sufficient description of the psychological state. Yet analysis of those qualities in the thing that cause us to make our pleasure a quality of it would supplement the definition sufficiently and completely in the sense of our own formula. Why do we regard pleasure as the quality of a thing? Because there is something in the thing that makes us spread, as it were, our pleasure upon it. This is that which fixates us, arrests us, upon it, — which can be only the elements that make for repose.

Guyau, however, comes nearest to our point of view. " The beautiful is a perception or an action which stimulates life within us under its three forms simultaneously (i. e., sensibility, intelligence, and will) and produces pleasure by the swift consciousness of this general stimulation." [1] It is from this general stimulation that Guyau explains the æsthetic effect of his famous drink of milk among mountain scenes. But such general stimulation

[1] *Problèmes de l'Esthétique Contemporaine*, 1902, p. 77.

might accompany successful action of any kind, and thus the moral and the æsthetic would fall together. That M. Guyau is so successful in his analysis is due rather to the fact that just this diffused stimulation is likely to come from such exercise as is characterized by the mutual checking of antagonistic impulses producing an equilibrium. The diffusion of stimulation would be our formula for the æsthetic state only if interpreted as stimulation arresting action.

The diffusion of stimulation, the equilibrium of impulses, life-enhancement through repose! — this is the æsthetic experience. But how, then, it will be asked, are we to interpret the temporal arts? A picture or a statue may be understood through this formula, but hardly a drama or a symphony. If the form of the one is symmetry, hidden or not, would not the form of the other be represented by a straight line? That which has beginning, middle, and end is not static but dynamic.

Let us consider once more the concept of equilibrium. Inhibition of action through antagonistic impulses, or action returning upon itself, we have defined it; and the line cannot be drawn sharply between these types. The visual analogue for equilibrium may be either symmetrical figure or circle; the excursion from the centre may be either the swing of the pendulum or the sweep of the planet. The *return* is the essential. Now it is a commonplace of criticism — though the significance of the dictum has never been sufficiently seen — that the great drama, novel, or symphony does return upon itself. The excursion is merely longer, of a different order of impulses from that of the picture. The last note is the only possible answer to the first; it contains the first. The last scene has meaning only as the satisfaction of the first. The measure of the perfection of a work of temporal art is thus its *implicit* character. The end is contained in the beginning — that is the meaning of "inevitableness."

That the constraining power of drama or symphony is just this sense of urgency, of compulsion, from one point to another, is but confirmation of this view. The temporal art tries ever to pass from first to last, which is first. It yearns for unity. The dynamic movement of the temporal arts is cyclic, which is ultimately static, of the nature of equilibrium. It is only in the wideness of the sweep that the dynamic repose of poetry and music differs from the static activity of picture and statue.

Thus the Nature of Beauty is in the relation of means to an end; the means, the possibilities of stimulation in the motor, visual, auditory, and purely ideal fields; the end, a moment of perfection, of self-complete unity of experience, of favorable stimulation with repose. Beauty is not perfection; but the beauty of an object lies in its permanent possibility of creating the perfect moment. The experience of this moment, the union of stimulation and repose, constitutes the unique æsthetic emotion.

III

THE ÆSTHETIC REPOSE

III

THE ÆSTHETIC REPOSE

THE popular interest in scientific truth has always had its hidden spring in a desire for the marvelous. The search for the philosopher's stone has done as much for chemistry as the legend of the elixir of life for exploration and geographical discovery. From the excitements of these suggestions of the occult, the world settled down into a reasonable understanding of the facts of which they were but the enlarged and grotesque shadows.

So it has been with physics and physiology, and so also, preëminently, with the science of mental life. Mesmerism, hypnotism, the facts of the alteration, the multiplicity, and the annihilation of personality have each brought us their moments of pleasurable terror, and passed thus into the field of general interest. But science can accept no broken chains. For all the thrill of mystery, we may not forget that the hypnotic state is but highly strung attention, — at the last turn of the screw, — and that the alternation of personality is after all no more than the highest power of variability of mood. In regard to the annihilation of the sense of personality, it may be said that no

connection with daily experience is at first apparent. Scientists, as well as the world at large, have
been inclined to look on the loss of the sense of
personality as pathological; and yet it may be
maintained that it is nevertheless the typical form
of those experiences we ourselves regard as the
most valuable.

The loss of personality! In that dread thought
there lies, to most of us, all the sting of death and
the victory of the grave. It seems, with such a
fate in store, that immortality were futile, and life
itself a mockery. Yet the idea, when dwelt upon,
assumes an aspect of strange familiarity; it is an
old friend, after all. Can we deny that all our
sweetest hours are those of self-forgetfulness? The
language of emotion, religious, æsthetic, intellectually creative, testifies clearly to the fading of the
consciousness of self as feeling nears the white
heat. Not only in the speechless, stark immobility
of the pathological "case," but in all the stages of
religious ecstasy, æsthetic pleasure, and creative
inspiration, is to be traced what we know as the
loss of the feeling of self. Bernard of Clairvaux
dwells on "that ecstasy of deification in which the
individual disappears in the eternal essence as the
drop of water in a cask of wine." Says Meister
Eckhart, "Thou shalt sink away from thy selfhood, thou shalt flow into His self-possession, the
very thought of Thine shall melt into His Mine;"
and St. Teresa, "The soul, in thus searching for

its God, feels with a very lively and very sweet
pleasure that it is fainting almost quite away."

Still more striking is the language of æsthetic
emotion. Philosopher and poet have but one expression for the universal experience. Says Keats
in the " Ode to a Nightingale : " —

> " My heart aches, and a drowsy numbness pains
>   My sense as though of hemlock I had drunk,
> Or emptied some dull opiate to the drains
>   One minute past, and Lethewards had sunk :
> 'T is not through envy of thy happy lot,
>   But being too happy in thy happiness."

And in Schopenhauer we read that he who con-
templates the beautiful " forgets even his individuality, his will, and only continues to exist as the
pure subject, the clear mirror of the object."

But not only the religious enthusiast and the
worshiper of beauty " lose themselves " in ecstasy.
The " fine frenzy " of the thinker is typical. From
Archimedes, whose life paid the forfeit of his impersonal absorption ; from Socrates, musing in one
spot from dawn to dawn, to Newton and Goethe,
there is but one form of the highest effort to pene-
trate and to create. Emerson is right in saying of
the genius, " His greatness consists in the fullness
in which an ecstatic state is realized in him."

The temporary evaporation of the consciousness
of one's own personality is then decidedly not a
pathological experience. It seems the condition,
indeed, and recognized as such in popular judg-

ment, of the deepest feeling and the highest achievement. Perhaps it is the very assumption of this condition in our daily thoughts that has veiled the psychological problem it presents. We opine, easily enough, that great deeds are done in forgetfulness of self. But why should we forget ourselves in doing great deeds? Why not as well feel in every act its reverberation on the self, — the renewed assurance that it is *I* who can? Why not, in each æsthetic thrill, awake anew to the consciousness of myself as ruler in a realm of beauty? Why not, in the rush of intellectual production, glory that " my mind to me a kingdom is "? And yet the facts are otherwise: in proportion to the intensity and value of the experience is its approach to the objective, the impersonal, the ecstatic state. Then how explain this anomaly? Why should religious, æsthetic, and intellectual emotion be accompanied in varying degrees by the loss of self-consciousness? Why should the sense of personality play us so strange a trick as to vanish, at the moment of seemingly greatest power, in the very shadow of its own glory?

If now we put the most obvious question, and ask, in explanation of its escapades, what the true nature of this personality is, we shall find ourselves quite out of our reckoning on the vast sea of metaphysics. To know what personality *is*, " root and all, and all in all," is to " know what God and man is." Fortunately, our problem is much more simple.

It is not the personality itself, its reality, its meaning, that vanishes; no, nor even the psychological system of dispositions. We remain, in such a moment of ecstasy, as persons, what we were before. It is the *feeling* of personality that has faded; and to find out in what this will-o'-the-wisp feeling of personality resides is a task wholly within the powers of psychological analysis. Let no one object that the depth and value of experience seem to disintegrate under the psychologist's microscope. The place of the full-orbed personality in a world of noble ends is not affected by the possibility that the centre of its conscious crystallization may be found in a single sensation.

The explanation, then, of this apparent inconsistency — the fading away of self in the midst of certain most important experiences — must lie in the nature of the feeling of personality. What is that feeling? On what is it based? How can it be described? The difficulties of introspection have led many to deny the possibility of such self-fixation. The fleeting moment passes, and we grasp only an idea or a feeling; the Ego has slipped away like a drop of mercury under the fingers. Like the hero of the German poet, who wanted his queue in front,

> "Then round and round, and out and in,
>   All day that puzzled sage did spin;
>   In vain; it mattered not a pin;
>   The pigtail hung behind him,"

when I turn round upon myself to catch myself in the act of thinking, I can never lay hold on anything but a sensation. I may peel off, like the leaves of an artichoke, my social self, — my possessions and positions, my friends, my relatives; my active self, — my books and implements of work; my clothes; even my flesh, and sit in my bones, like Sydney Smith, — the *I* in me retreating ever to an inner citadel; but I must stop with the feeling that something moves in there. That is not what my self *is*, but what the elusive sprite feels like when I have got my finger on him. In daily experience, however, it is unnecessary to proceed to such extremities. The self, at a given moment of consciousness, is felt as one group of elements which form a background of consciousness as over against another group of elements which form a foreground. The second group is, we say, before the attention, and is not at that moment felt as self; while the first group is vague, undifferentiated, not attended to, but felt. Any element in this background can detach itself and come into the foreground of attention. I become conscious at this moment, for instance, of the weight of my shoulders as they rest on the back of my chair: that sensation, however, belongs to my self no more than does the sensation of the smoothness of the paper on which my hand rests. I know I am a self, because I can pass, so to speak, between the foreground and the background of my consciousness. It is the feeling of transition that gives me the negative and positive of my circuit ; and this feeling of transition, hunted to its lair, reveals itself as nothing more nor less than a motor sensation felt in the sense organs which adapt themselves to the new conditions. I look on that picture and on this, and know that they are two, because the change in the adaptation of my sense organs to their objects has been felt. I close my eyes and think of near and far, and it is the change in the sensations from my eye muscles that tells me I have passed between the two ; or, to express it otherwise, that it is in me the two have succeeded each other. While the self in its widest sense, therefore, is co-extensive with consciousness, the distinctive feeling of self as opposed to the elements in consciousness which represent the outer world is based on those bodily sensations which are connected with the relations of objects. My world — the foreground of my consciousness — would fall in on me and crush me, if I could not hold it off by just this power to feel it different from my background ; and it is felt as different through the motor sensations involved in the change of my sense organs in passing from one to the other. The condition of the feeling of transition, and hence of the feeling of personality, is then the presence in consciousness of at least two possible objects of attention ; and the formal consciousness of self might be schematized as a straight line connecting two points, in which one point represents the foreground, and the other the background, of consciousness.

If we now accept this view, and ask under what conditions the sense of self may be lost, the answer is at once suggested. It will happen when the "two-ness" disappears, so that the line connecting and separating the two objects in our scheme drops out or is indefinitely decreased. When background or foreground tends to disappear or to merge either into the other, or when background or foreground makes an indissoluble unity or unbreakable circle, the content of consciousness approaches absolute unity. There is no "relating" to be done, no "transition" to be made. The condition, then, for the feeling of personality is no longer present, and there results a feeling of complete unity with the object of attention; and if this object of attention is itself without parts or differences, there results an empty void, Nirvana.

Suppose that I gaze, motionless, at a single bright light until all my bodily sensations have faded. Then one of the "points" in our scheme has dropped out. In my mind there reigns but one thought. The transition feeling goes, for there is nothing to be "related." Now "it is one blaze, about me and within me;" I *am* that light, and myself no longer. My consciousness is a unit or a blank, as you please. If you say that I am self-hypnotized, I may reply that I have simply ceased to feel myself different from the content of my consciousness, because that content has ceased to allow a transition between its terms.

This is, however, not the only possible form of the disappearance of our " twoness," and the resulting loss of the self-feeling. When the sequence of objects in consciousness is so rapid that the feeling of transition, expressed in motor terms, drops below the threshold of sensation, the feeling of self again fades. Think, for instance, of the Bacchanal orgies. The votary of Dionysus, dancing, shrieking, tearing at his hair and at his garments, lost in the lightning change of his sensations all power of relating them. His mind was ringed in a whirling circle, every point of which merged into the next without possibility of differentiation. And since he could feel no transition periods, he could feel *himself* no longer ; he was one with the content of his consciousness, which consciousness was no less a unit than our bright light aforesaid, just as a circle is as truly a unit as a point. The priest of Dionysus must have felt himself only a dancing, shouting thing, one with the world without, " whirled round in earth's diurnal course with rocks and stones and trees." And how perfectly the ancient belief fits our psychophysical analysis ! The Bacchic enthusiast believed himself possessed with the very ecstasy of the spirit of nature. His inspired madness was the presence of the god who descended upon him, — the god of the vine, of spring ; the rising sap, the rushing stream, the bursting leaf, the rippling

song, all the life of flowing things, they were he!
" αὐτίκα γᾶ πᾶσα χορεύσει," was the cry, — " soon the
whole earth will dance and sing! "

Yes, this breaking down of barriers, this melt-
ing of the personality into its surroundings, this
strange and sweet self-abandonment must have its
source in just the disappearance of the sensation of
adjustment, on which the feeling of personality is
based. But how can it be, we have to ask, that
a principle so barren of emotional significance
should account for the ecstasy of religious emotion,
of æsthetic delight, of creative inspiration? It is
not, however, religion or beauty or genius that is the
object of our inquiry at this moment, but simply
the common element in the experience of each of
these which we know as the disappearance of self-
feeling. How the circumstances peculiar to religious worship, æsthetic appreciation, and intellectual creation bring about the formal conditions of
the loss of personal feeling must be sought in a
more detailed analysis, and we shall then be able
to trace the source of the intensity of emotion in
these experiences. What, then, first of all, are the
steps by which priest and poet and thinker have
passed into the exaltation of selfless emotion? Fortunately, the passionate pilgrims to all three realms
of deep experience have been ever prodigal of
their confessions. The religious ecstasy, however,
embodies the most complete case, and allows
the clearest insight into the nature of the experi-

ence; and will therefore be dealt with at greatest length.

The typical religious enthusiast is the mystic. From Plotinus to Buddha, from Meister Eckhart to Emerson, the same doctrine has brought the same fruits of religious rapture. There is one God, and in contemplation of Him the soul becomes of his essence. Whether it is held, as by the Neoplatonists, that Being and Knowledge are one, that the procedure of the world out of God is a process of self-revelation, and the return of things into God a process of higher and higher intuition, and so the mystic experience an apprehension of the highest rather than a form of worship; or whether it is expressed as by the humble Béguine, Mechthild, — "My soul swims in the Being of God as a fish in water," — the kernel of the mystic's creed is the same. In ecstatic contemplation of God, and, in the higher states, in ecstatic union with Him, in sinking the individuality in the divine Being, is the only true life. Not all, it is true, who hold the doctrine have had the experience; not all can say with Eckhart or with Madame Guyon, " I have seen God in my own soul," or " I have become one with God." It is from the narratives and the counsels of perfection of these, the chosen, the initiate, who have passed beyond the veil, that light may be thrown on the psychological conditions of mystic ecstasy.

The most illuminating account of her actual mystical experiences is given by Madame Guyon, the first of the sect or school of the Quietists. This gentle Frenchwoman had a gift for psychological observation, and though her style is neither poetic nor philosophical, I may be pardoned for quoting at some length her naïve and lucid revelations. The following passages, beginning with an early religious experience, are taken almost at random from the pages of her autobiography : —

"These sermons made such an impression on my mind, and absorbed me so strongly in God, that I could not open my eyes nor hear what was said." "To hear Thy name, O my God, could put me into a profound prayer. . . . I could not see any longer the saints nor the Holy Virgin outside of God ; but I saw them all in Him, scarcely being able to distinguish them from Him. . . . I could not hear God nor our Lord Jesus Christ spoken of without being, as it were, outside of myself [*hors de moi*]. . . . Love seized me so strongly that I remained absorbed, in a profound silence and a peace that I cannot describe. I made ever new efforts, and I passed my life in beginning my prayers without being able to carry them through. . . . I could ask nothing for myself nor for another, nor wish anything but this divine will. . . . I do not believe that there could be in the world anything more simple and more unified. . . . It is a state of which one can say nothing more, because it evades all expression, — a state in which the creature is lost, engulfed. All is God, and the soul perceives only God. It has to strive no more for perfection, for growth, for approach to Him, for union. All is consummated in the unity, but in a manner so free, so natural, so easy, that the soul lives in and from God, as easily as the body lives from the air which it breathes. ... The spirit is empty, no more traversed by thoughts; nothing fills the void, which is no longer painful, and the soul finds in itself an immense capacity that nothing can either limit or destroy."

Can we fail to trace in these simple words the shadow of all religious exaltation that is based on faith alone? Madame Guyon is strung to a higher key than most of this dull and relaxed world; but she has struck the eternal note of contemplative worship. Such is the sense of union with the divine Spirit. Such are the thoughts and even the words of Dante, Eckhart, St. Teresa, the countless mystics of the Middle Age, and of the followers of Buddhism in its various shades, from the Ganges to the Charles. Two characteristics disengage themselves to view: the insistence on the unity of God — *in* whom alone the Holy Virgin and the saints are seen — from a psychological point of view only; and the mind's emptiness of thought in a state of religious ecstasy. But without further analysis, we may ask, as the disciples of the mystics have always done, how this state of blissful union is to be reached. They have always been minute in their prescriptions, and it is possible to derive therefrom what may be called the technique of the mystic procedure.

"The word mystic," to quote Walter Pater, "has been derived from a Greek word which signifies *to shut*, as if one *shut one's lips*, brooding on what cannot be uttered; but the Platonists themselves derive it rather from the act of *shutting the eyes*, that one may see the more, inwardly." Of such is the counsel of St. Luis de Granada, "Imitate the sportsman who hoods the falcon that it be made subservient to his rule;" and of another Spanish mystic, Pedro de Alcantara: "In meditation, let the person rouse himself from things temporal, and let him collect himself within himself. . . . Here let him hearken to the voice of God . . . as though there were no other in the world save God and himself." St. Teresa found happiness only in "shutting herself up within herself." Vocal prayer could not satisfy her, and she adopted mental prayer. The four stages of her experience — which she named "recollectedness," "quietude" (listening rather than speaking), "union" (blissful sleep with the faculties of the mind still), "ecstasy or rapture" — are but progressive steps in the sealing of the senses. The *yoga* of the Brahmins, which is the same as the "union" of the Cabalists, is made to depend upon the same conditions, — passivity, perseverance, solitude. The novice must arrest his breathing, and may meditate on mystic symbols alone, by way of reaching the formless, ineffable

Buddha. But it is useless to heap up evidence ; the inference is sufficiently clear.

The body is first brought into a state either of nervous instability or irritability by ascetic practices, or of nervous insensibility by the persistent withdrawal of all outer disturbance ; and the mind is fixed upon a single object, — the one God, the God eternal, absolute, indivisible. Recalling our former scheme for the conditions of the sense of personality, we shall see that we have here the two poles of consciousness. Then, as the tension is sharpened, what happens ? Under the artificial conditions of weakened nerves, of blank surroundings, the self-background drops. The feeling of transition disappears with the absence of related terms ; and the remaining, the positive pole of consciousness, is an undifferentiated Unity, with which the person must feel himself one. The feeling of personality is gone with that on which it rests, and its loss is joined with an overwhelming sense of union with the One, the Absolute, God !

The object of mystic contemplation is the One indivisible. But we can also think the One as the unity of all differences, the Circle of the Universe. Those natures also which, like Amiel's, are " bedazzled with the Infinite " and thirst for " totality " attain in their reveries to the same impersonal ecstasy. Amiel writes of a " night on the sandy shore of the North Sea, stretched at full length upon the beach, my eyes wandering over the Milky Way.

Will they ever return to me, those grandiose, im-
mortal, cosmogonic dreams, in which one seems to
carry the world in one's breast, to touch the stars,
to possess the Infinite!" The reverie of Sénancour, on the bank of the Lake of Bienne, quoted by
Matthew Arnold, reveals the same emotion: "Vast
consciousness of a nature everywhere greater than
we are, and everywhere impenetrable; all-embracing passion, ripened wisdom, delicious self-abandonment." In the coincidence of outer circumstance
— the lake, the North Sea, night, the attitude
of repose — may we not trace a dissolution of the
self-background, similar to that of the mystic worshiper? And in the Infinite, no less than in the
One, must the soul sink and melt into union with
it, because within it there is no determination, no
pause, and no change.

The contemplation of the One, however, is not
the only type of mystic ecstasy. That intoxication
of emotion which seizes upon the negro camp meeting of to-day, as it did upon the Delphic priestesses
two thousand years ago, seems at first glance to
have nothing in common psychologically with the
blessed nothingness of Gautama and Meister Eckhart. But the loss of the feeling of personality
and the sense of possession by a divine spirit are
the same. How, then, is this state reached? By
means, I believe, which recall the general formula
for the disappearance of self-feeling. To repeat
the monosyllable *om* (Brahm) ten thousand times;

to circle interminably, chanting the while, about a sacred fire; to listen to the monotonous magic drum; to whirl the body about; to rock to and fro on the knees, vociferating prayers, are methods which enable the members of the respective sects in which they are practiced either to enter, as they say, into the Eternal Being, or to become informed with it through the negation of the self. The sense of personality, at any rate, is more or less completely lost, and the ecstasy takes a form more or less passionate, according as the worshiper depends on the rapidity rather than on the monotony of his excitations. Here, again, the self-background drops, inasmuch as every rhythmical movement tends to become automatic, and then unconscious. Thus what we are wont to call the inspired madness of the Delphic priestesses was less the expression of ecstasy than the means of its excitation. Perpetual motion, as well as eternal rest, may bring about the engulfment of the self in the object. The most diverse types of religious emotions, *in so far as they present variations in the degree of self-consciousness*, are thus seen to be reducible to the same psychological basis. The circle, no less than the point, is the symbol of the One, and the "devouring unity" that lays hold on consciousness from the loss of the feeling of transition comes in the unrest of enthusiasm no less than in the blissful nothing of Nirvana.

At this point, I am sure, the reader will interpose

a protest. Is, then, the mystery of self-abandonment to the highest to be shared with the meanest
of fanatics? Are the rapture of Dante and the
trance of the Omphalopsychi sprung from the same
root? There is no occasion, however, for the revolt
of sentiment because we fail to emphasize here the
important differences in the emotional character
and value of the states in question. What interests
us is only one aspect which they have in common,
the surrender of the sense of personality. That is
based on formal relations of the elements of consciousness, and the explanation of its disappearance
applies as well to the whirling dervish as to the
converts of a revivalist preacher.

The mystic, then, need only shut his senses to the
world, and contemplate the One. Subject fuses
with object, and he feels himself melt into the Infinite. But such experience is not the exclusive
property of the religious enthusiast. The worshiper
of beauty has given evidence of the same feelings. And yet, in his æsthetic rapture, the latter
dwells with deliberation on his delights, and while
luxuriating in the infinite labyrinths of beauty can
scarcely be described as musing on an undifferentiated Unity. So far, at least, it does not appear
that our formula applies to æsthetic feeling.

Æsthetic feeling arises in the contemplation of a
beautiful object. But what makes an object beautiful? To go still further back, just what, psychologically, does contemplation mean? To contem-

plate an object is to dwell on the idea or image of it, and to dwell upon an idea means to carry it out incipiently. We may go even further, and say it is the carrying out by virtue of which we grasp the idea. How do we think of a tall pine-tree ? By sweeping our eyes up and down its length, and out to the ends of its branches ; and if we are forbidden to use our eye muscles even infinitesimally, then we cannot think of the visual image. In short, we perceive an object in space by carrying out its motor suggestions ; more technically expressed, by virtue of a complex of motor impulses aroused by it ; more briefly, by incipiently imitating it. Contemplation is inner imitation.

Now a beautiful object is first of all a unified object ; why this must be so has been considered in the preceding chapter. In it all impulses of soul and sense are bound to react upon one another, and to lead back to one another. And all the elements, which in contemplation we reproduce in the form of motor impulses, are bound to make a closed circle of these suggested energies. The symmetrical picture calls out a set of motor impulses which " balance," — a system of energies reacting on one centre ; the sonnet takes us out on one wave of rhythm and of thought, to bring us back on another to the same point ; the sonata does the same in melody. In the " whirling circle " of the drama, not a word or an act that is not indissolubly linked with before and after. Thus the unity of a work of art makes of the system of suggested energies which form the foreground of attention an impregnable, an invulnerable circle.

Not only, however, are we held in equilibrium in the object of attention; we cannot connect with it our self-background, for the will cannot act on the object of æsthetic feeling. We cannot eat the grapes of Apelles or embrace the Galatea of Pygmalion; we cannot rescue Ophelia or enlighten Juliet; and of impulse to interfere, to connect the scene with ourselves, we have none. But this is a less important factor in the situation. That the house is dark, the audience silent, and all motor impulses outside of the æsthetic circle stifled, is, too, only a superficial, and, so to speak, a negative condition. The real ground of the possibility of a momentary self-annihilation lies in the fact that all incitements to motor impulse — except those which belong to the indissoluble ring of the object itself — have been shut out by the perfection of unity to which the æsthetic object (here the drama) has been brought. The background fades; the foreground satisfies, incites no movement; and with the disappearance of the possibility of action which would connect the two, fades also that which dwells in this feeling of transition,—the sense of personality. The depth of æsthetic feeling lies not in the worthy countryman who interrupts the play with cries for justice on the villain, but in him who creates the drama again with the poet, who lives over again in

himself each of the thrills of emotion passing before
him, and loses himself in their web. The object is
a unity or our whirling circle of impulses, as you
like to phrase it. At any rate, out of that unity the
soul does not return upon itself; it remains one
with it in the truest sense.

The loss of the sense of personality is an integral
part of the æsthetic experience; and we have seen
how it is a necessary psychological effect of the unity
of the object. From another point of view it may
be said that the unity of the object is constituted
just by the inhibition of all tendency to movement
through the balance or centrality of impulses suggested by it. In other words, the balance of impulses makes us feel the object a unity. And this
balance of impulses, this inhibition of movement,
corresponding to unity, is what we know as æsthetic
repose. Thus the conditions of æsthetic repose and
of the loss of self-feeling are the same. In fact, it
might be said that, within this realm, the two conceptions are identical. The true æsthetic repose is
just that perfect rest in the beautiful object which
is the essence of the loss of the sense of personality.

Subtler and rarer, again, than the raptures of
mysticism and of beauty worship is the ecstasy
of intellectual production; yet the "clean, clear
joy of creation," as Kipling names it, is not less
to be grouped with those precious experiences in
which the self is sloughed away, and the soul at
one with its content. I speak, of course, of intel-

lectual production in full swing, in the momentum of success. The travail of soul over apparently hopeless difficulties or in the working out of indifferent details takes place not only in full self-consciousness, but in self-disgust; there we can take Carlyle to witness. But in the higher stages the fixation of truth and the appreciation of beauty are accompanied by the same extinction of the feeling of individuality. Of testimony we have enough and to spare. I need not fill these pages with confessions and anecdotes of the ecstatical state in which all great deeds of art and science are done. The question is rather to understand and explain it on the basis of the formal scheme to which we have found the religious and the æsthetic attitudes to conform.

Jean Paul says somewhere that, however laborious the completion of a great work, its conception came as a whole, — in one flash. We remember the dreams of Schiller in front of his red curtain and the resulting *musikalische Stimmung*, — formless, undirected, out of which his poem shaped itself ; the half-somnambulic state of Goethe and his frantic haste in fixation of the vision, in which he dared not even stop to put his paper straight, but wrote over the corners quite ruthlessly. Henner once said to a painter who mourned that he had done nothing on his picture for the Salon, though he saw it before him, " What ! You see your picture ! Then it is done. You can paint it in an hour." If all these traditions be true, they are significant; and the necessary conditions of such composition seem to be highly analogous to those of the æsthetic emotion. We have, first of all, a lack of outward stimulation, and therefore possible disappearance of the background. How much better have most poets written in a garret than in a boudoir! Goethe's bare little room in the garden house at Weimar testifies to the severe conditions his genius found necessary. Tranquillity of the background is the condition of self-absorption, or — and this point seems to me worth emphasizing — a closed circle of outer activities. I have never believed, for instance, in the case of the old tale of Walter Scott and the button, that it was the surprise of his loss that tied the tongue of the future author's rival. The poor head scholar had simply made for himself a transitionless experience with that twirling button, and could then sink his consciousness in its object, — at that moment the master's questions. It is with many of us a familiar experience, that of not being able to think unless in constant motion. Translated into our psychological scheme, the efficiency of these movements would be explained thus: Given the "whirling circles," — the background of continuous movement sensations, which finally dropped out of consciousness, and the foreground of continuous thought, — the first protected, so to speak, the second, since they were mutually exclusive, and what broke the one destroyed the other.

But to return from this digression, a background fading into nothingness, either as rest or as a closed circle of automatic movements, is the first condition of the ecstasy of mental production. The second is given in the character of its object. The object of high intellectual creation is a unity, — a perfect whole, revealed, as Jean Paul says, in a single movement of genius. Within the enchanted circle of his creation, the thinker is absorbed, because here too all his impulses are turned to one end, in relation to which nothing else exists.

I am aware that many will see a sharp distinction here between the work of the creator or discoverer in science and the artist. They may maintain, in Schopenhauer's phrase, that the aim and end of science is just the connection of objects in the service of the will of the individual, and hence transition between the various terms is constant; while art, on the other hand, indeed isolates its object, and so drops transitions. But I think where we speak of "connection" thus, we mean the larger sweep of law. If the thinker looks beyond his special problem at all, it is, like Buddha, to "fix his eyes upon the chain of causation." The scientist of imagination sees his work under the form of eternity, as one link of that endless chain, one atom in that vortex of almighty purposes, which science will need all time to reveal. For him it is either one question, closed within itself by its own answer, or it is the Infinite Law of the Universe,

— the point or the circle. From all points of view, then, the object of creation in art or science is a girdle of impulses from which the mind may not stray. The two conditions of our formal scheme are given : a term which disappears, and one which is a perfect whole. Transition between background and foreground of attention is no longer possible, because the background has dropped. Between the objects of attention in the foreground it has no meaning, because the foreground is an indissoluble unity. With that object the self must feel itself one, since the distinctive self-feeling has disappeared with the opportunity for transition.

We have thus swung around the circle of mystical, æsthetic, and creative emotion, and we have found a single formula to apply, and a single explanation to avail for the loss of personality. The conditions of such experiences bring about the disappearance of one term, and the impregnable unity of the other. Without transition between two terms in consciousness, two objects of attention, the loss of the feeling of personality takes place according to natural psychological laws. It is no longer a mystery that in intense experience the feeling of personality dissolves.

One point, however, does remain still unexplained, — the bliss of self-abandonment. Whence are the definiteness and intensity of the religious and æsthetic emotions ? The surrender of the sense of personality, it seems, is based on purely formal relations of the elements of consciousness, common to all three groups of the analyzed emotions. Yet it is precisely with a fading of self-feeling that intensity and definiteness deepen. But how can different and emotionally significant feelings arise from a single formal process? How can the worship of God become ecstatic joy through the loss of personality? The solution of this apparent paradox is demanded not only in logic, but also by those who would wish to see the religious trance distinguished also in its origin from those of baser content.

But it is, after all, the formal nature of the phenomenon that gives us light. If variation in the degree of self-feeling is the common factor, and the disappearance of the transition-feeling its cause, then the lowest member of the scale, in which the loss of self-feeling takes place with mathematical completeness, must be included. That is the hypnotic trance. It is not necessary at this place to emphasize the fact that our theory, if accepted, would constitute a theory and a definition also of hypnotism. Of interest to our inquiry is merely a characteristic mark of the hypnotic state, — its tremendous suggestibility. Why is this? Our theory would answer that all impulses are held in equilibrium, and that an external suggestion has thus no rivals. Whatever the cause, this last is at any rate the fact. All suggestions seem to double in emotional value. Tell the hypnotic subject that he is sailing up the Rhine, and the most vivid admiration is in his aspect; he gazes in heart-felt devotion if it is a pretty girl he is bid to look at; he quaffs a glass of water with livelier delight than he would show for the draught of Château Yquem of which he is led to think.

Now in religious and æsthetic experience there is brought about the same equilibrium or unity of impulses, resulting in analogous loss of self-feeling. But it is a most interesting fact that the *form* of the contemplated object is the cause of this arrest and repose. God, the circle of the Infinite, the Eternal One, enter into play as "unity" alone. What, then, of the content? After the analogy of the extreme case, the content — that is, emotional value and definite emotional tone — takes the place of the external suggestion. Under just the conditions of the religious trance, the element of reverence, of joyous sentiment, is able suddenly to take on a more vivid aspect. It may not be that the emotion itself is greater, but it now holds the field. It may not be that it is more intense, but the intensity of concentration which takes on its color makes it seem so. The "rapture" is just the sense of being caught up into union with the highest; the joy of the rapture is the joy of every thought of God, here left free to brighten into ecstasy; and its "revelation-value" is again the sense of immediate union with a Being the intellectual concept of whom is immensely vivified.

So may be analyzed the æsthetic ecstasy. The tension of those mutually antagonistic impulses which make balance, and so unity, and so the conditions for loss of sense of self, clears the way for tasting the full savor of pleasure in bright color, flowing line, exquisite tone-sequence, moving thought. Many a commonplace experience, says M. Souriau, suddenly takes on a charm when seen in the arrested æsthetic vision. " Every one can have observed that an object in itself agreeable to look on, like a bouquet of flowers, or the fresh face of a young girl, takes on a sort of magic and supernatural beauty if we regard it mechanically while listening to music." [1] The intensity of concentration caused by the unity of form fuses with this suggested vividness of feeling from content and material, and the whole is felt as intensity of æsthetic emotion. The Sistine Madonna would not strike so deep in feeling were it less crystalline in its unity, less trance-like in its repose, and so less enchanting in its suggestion.

So it is not only the man of achievement who sees but one thing at a time. To enter intensely into any ideal experience means to be blind to all others. One must lose one's own soul to gain the world, and none who enter and return from the paradise of selfless ecstasy will question that it is gained. It may be that personality is a hindrance and a barrier, and that we are only truly in har-

[1] P. Souriau, *La Suggestion en l'Art.*

mony with the secret of our own existence when we cease to set ourselves over against the world. Nevertheless, the sense of individuality is a possession for which the most of mankind would pay the price, if it must be paid, even of eternal suffering. The delicious hour of fusion with the universe is precious, so it seems to us now, just because we can return from it to our own nest, and, close and warm there, count up our happiness. The fragmentariness and multiplicity of life are, then, the saving of the sense of selfhood, and we must indeed

> "Rejoice that man is hurled
> From change to change unceasingly,
> His soul's wings never furled."

IV

THE BEAUTY OF FINE ART

IV

A. THE BEAUTY OF VISUAL FORM

I

IN what consists the Beauty of Visual Form? The older writers on what we now know as the science of art did not ask themselves this question. Although we are accustomed to hear that order, symmetry, unity in variety, was the Greek, and in particular the Platonic, formula for beauty, we observe, on examining the passages cited in evidence, that it is rather the moral quality appertaining to these characteristics that determines them as beautiful; symmetry is beautiful, because harmonious, and inducing order and self-restraint. Aristotle's single pronouncement in the sense of our question is the dictum: there is no beauty without a certain magnitude. Lessing, in his "Laocoon," really the first modern treatise in æsthetics, discusses the excellences of painting and poetry, but deals with visible beauty as if it were a fixed quality, understood when referred to, like color. This is undoubtedly due to his unconscious reference of beauty to the human form alone; a reference which he would have denied, but which influences his whole æsthetic theory. In speaking of a beautiful picture, for instance, he would have meant first of all the representation of beautiful persons in it, hardly at all that essential beauty of the picture as painting, to which every inch of the canvas is alike precious. It is clear to us now, however, that the beauty of the human form is the most obscure of all possible cases, complex in itself, and overlaid and involved as it is with innumerable interests and motives of extra-æsthetic character. Beauty in simple forms must be our first study; and great credit is due to Hogarth for having propounded in his " Analysis of Beauty " the simple question, — what makes the quality of beauty to the eye?

But in visible beauty, the æsthetic value of pure form is not the only element involved : or at least it must be settled whether or not it is the only element involved. If in a work of art, as we believe, what belongs to its excellence belongs to its beauty, we may not applaud one painter, for instance, for his marvelous color-schemes, another for his expression of emotion, another for his delineation of character, without acknowledging that expression of character and emotion come within our concept of visible beauty. Franz von Lenbach was once asked what he thought likely to be the fate of his own work. " As for that," he replied, " I think I may possibly have a chance of living; but *only* if Individualization or Characterization be deemed to constitute a quality of permanent value in a picture. This, however, I shall never know, for it can only be adjudged by posterity. If that verdict should prove unfavorable, then my work, too, will perish with the rest, — for it cannot compare on their lines with the great masters of the past." That this is indeed an issue is shown by the contrasting opinion of the critic who exclaimed before a portrait, " Think away the head and face, and you will have a wonderful effect of color!" The analysis of visible beauty accordingly resolves itself into the explanation of the beauty of form (including shape and color) and the fixing in relation thereto of other factors.

The most difficult part of our task is indeed behind us. We have already defined Beauty in general: we have outlined in a preceding essay the abstract æsthetic demands, and we have now only to ask through what psychological means these demands can be and are in fact met. In other words we have to show that what we intensely feel as Beauty can and does exemplify these principles, and through them is explained and accounted for. Beauty has been defined as that combination of qualities in the object which brings about a union of stimulation and repose in the enjoyer. How must this be interpreted with reference to the particular facts of visual form ?

The most immediate reference is naturally to the sense organ itself; and the first question is therefore as to the favorable stimulations of the eye. What, in general, does the eye demand of its object ?

II

The simplest element of visual experience is of course found in light and color, the sensation of the eye as such. Yet there is no branch of æsthetic which is so incomplete. We know that the sensation of light or color, if not too weak or too violent, is in itself pleasing. The bright, the glittering, shining object, so long as it is not painful, is pleasantly stimulating. Gems, tinsel, lacquer, polish, testify to this taste, from the most primitive to the most civilized man. Color, too, if distinct, not over-bright, nor too much extended in field, is in itself pleasing. The single colors have been the object of comparatively little study. Experiment seems to show that the colors containing most brightness — white, red, and yellow — are preferred. Baldwin, in his "dynamogenic" experiments,[1] based on "the view that the infant's hand movements in reaching or grasping are the best index of the kind and intensity of its sensory experiences," finds that the colors range themselves in order of attractiveness, blue, white, red, green, brown. Further corrections lay more emphasis upon the white. Yellow was not included in the experiments. Cohn's results, which show a relative dislike of yellow, are contradicted by other observers, nota-

[1] *Mental Development in the Child and the Race*, 1895, pp. 39, 50, ff.

bly Major and Baker,[1] and (unpublished) experiments of my own, including the æsthetic preferences
of seven or eight different sets of students at Rad-
cliffe and Wellesley colleges. Experiments of this
kind are particularly difficult, inasmuch as the
material, usually colored paper, varies considerably
from the spectral color, and differences in saturation, hue, and brightness make great differences in
the results, while the feeling-tone of association, individual or racial, very often intrudes. But other
things being equal, the bright, the clear, the satu-
rated color is relatively more pleasing, and white,
red, and yellow seem especially preferred.

Now, according to the Hering theory of color,
white, red, and yellow are the so-called " dissimilating " colors in the three pairs, white-black, red-
green, and yellow-blue, corresponding to three hypothetical visual substances in the retina. These
substances, that is, in undergoing a kind of chemi-
cal disintegration under the action of light-rays,
are supposed to give the sensations white, red, or
yellow respectively, and in renewing themselves
again to give the sensations of black, green, and
blue. The dissimilating process seems to bring
about stronger reactions on the physiological side,
as if it were a more exciting process. Thus it is
found [2] that as measured by the increase in strength

---

[1] E. S. Baker, *Univ. of Toronto Studies, Psychol. Series*, No. 4 ;
J. Cohn, *Philos. Studien*, vol. x ; Major, *Amer. Journ. of Psychol.*,
vol. vii.

[2] Ch. Féré, *Sensation et Mouvement*, 1887, p. 80.

of the hand grip under the stimulation of the respective colors, red has particularly exciting qualities, but the other colors have an analogous effect, lessening, however, with the descent from red to violet. The pleasure in bright red, or yellow, for instance, may thus well be the feeling-tone arising in the purely physiological effect of the color. If red works like a trumpet call, while blue calms and cools, and if red is preferred to blue, it is because a sharp stimulation is so felt, and so preferred.

The question of the demands of the eye in color combination is still more complicated. It has been traditional to consider the complementaries black-white, red-green, blue-yellow, and the other pairs resulting from the mixtures of these as the best combinations. The physiological explanation is of course found in the relief and refreshment to the organs in successive alternation of the processes of assimilation and dissimilation, and objectively in the reinforcement, through this stronger functioning of the retina, of the complementary colors themselves. This tendency to mutual aid is shown in the familiar experiment of fixating for some moments a colored object, say red, and then transferring the gaze to a white or gray expanse. The image of the object appears thereon in the complementary green. *Per contra*, the most complete lack of contrast makes the most unpleasing combination, because instead of a refreshing alternation of processes in the retina, a fatiguing repetition results. Red and orange (red-yellow), or red and purple (red-blue), successively stimulate the red-process with most evil effect.

This contrast theory should, however, not be interpreted too narrowly. There are pairs of so-called complementaries which make a very crude, harsh, even painful impression. The theory is happily supplemented by showing [1] that the ideal combination involves all three contrast factors, hue, saturation, and brightness. Contrast of saturation or brightness within the same hue is also pleasant. For any two qualities of the color circle, in fact, there can be found degrees of saturation and brightness in which they will form an agreeable combination, and this pleasing effect will be based on some form of contrast. But the absolute and relative extension and the space-form of the components have also a great influence on the pleasurableness of combinations.

Further rules can hardly be given; but the results of various observers [2] seem to show that the best combinations lie, as already said, among the complementaries, or among those pairs nearer together in the color circle than complementaries, which are "warmer." The reason for this last is

---

[1] A. Kirschmann, "Die psychol.-æsthet. Bedeutung des Licht und Farbencontrastes," *Philos. Studien*, vol. vii.

[2] Chevreul, *De la Loi du Contraste Simultané des Couleurs.* E. S. Baker, *op. cit.*

that, in Chevreul's phraseology, combinations of cold colors change each other's peculiar hue the most, and of warm colors the least; because the complementaries of these cold colors are "warm," i. e. bright, and each, appearing on the field of the neighboring cold color, seems to fade it out; while the complementaries of the juxtaposed warm colors are not bright, and do not have sufficient strength to affect their neighbors at all. With a combination of blue and green for instance, a yellow shade would appear in the green and a red in the blue. Such a result fails to satisfy the demand, already touched on, for purity and homogeneity of color, — that is, for unimpeded seeing of color.

What significance have these abstract principles of beauty in the combination of colors for representative art? In the choice of objects with a definite local color, of course, these laws will be found operative. A scheme of blues and yellows is likely to be more effective than one of reds and violets. If we analyze the masterpieces of coloring, we shall find that what we at first supposed to be the wonderful single effects of color is really the result of juxtapositions which bring out each color to its highest power.

III

While all this may be true, however, the most important question has not yet been asked. Is truth of color in representative art the same thing as beauty of color? It might be said that the whole procedure of the so-called Impressionist school, in fact the whole trend of the modern treatment of color, took their identity for granted. Yet we must discriminate. Truth of color may be truth to the local color of the given objects, alone or together; in this case we should have to say that beauty did or did not exist in the picture, according as it did or did not exist in the original combination. A red hat on a purple chair would set one's teeth on edge, in model or picture. Secondly, truth of color may be truth to the modifications of the enveloping light, and in this case truth would make for beauty. For the colors of any given scene are in general not colors which the objects themselves, if isolated, would have, but the colors which the eye itself is forced to see. The bluish shadow of an object in bright sunlight (yellowish light) is only an expression of the law that in the neighborhood of a colored object we see its complementary color. If such an effect is reproduced in a picture, it gives the same relief to the eye which the original effect showed the need of. The eye fatigued with yellow sees blue; so if the blue is really supplied in the picture, it is not only true, but on the road to beauty, because meeting the eye's demand. The older methods of painting gave the local color of an object, with an admixture of white for the lights, and a warm dark for the shadows; the modern — which had been touched on, indeed, sporadically, by Perugino and Vermeer, for instance, — gives in the shadow the complementary color of the object combined with that of the light falling upon it — all conditions of favorable stimulation.

Further favorable stimulation of the eye is given in the method of the Impressionists in treating "values," that is, comparative relations of light and shade. The real tones of objects including the sky, light, etc., can never be reproduced. The older schools, conscious of this, were satisfied to paint in a scale of correspondence, in which the relative values were fairly kept. But even by that means, the great differences of intensity could not be given, for the brightest spot of any painting is never more than sixty-six times brighter than the darkest, while the gray sky on a dull rainy day is four hundred and twenty times brighter than a white painted cross-bar of a window seen against the sky as background.[1] There were various ways of combating this difficulty. Rembrandt, for instance, as Kirschmann tells us, chose the sombre brown tone, "not out of caprice or an inclination for mystic dreaming (Fromentin), but because the yellow and orange side of the color-manifold admits of the greatest number of intervals between full saturation and the darkest shade." The precursors of the Impressionists, on the other hand, succeeded in painting absolute

[1] Kirschmann, *Univ. of Toronto Studies, Pyschol. Series*, No. 4, p. 20.

values, confining themselves to a very limited gamut; for this reason the first landscapes of the school were all gray-green, dull, cloudy. But Monet did not stop there. He painted the *absolute values* of objects *in shade* on a sunny day, which of course demands the brightest possibilities of the palette, and got the lighted objects themselves as nearly as he could, — thus destroying the relative values, but getting an extraordinarily joyous and glowing effect; and one, too, of unexpected verisimilitude, for it would seem that in a sunlit scene we are really attentive to the shaded objects alone, and what becomes of the others does not so much matter. This effect was made still more possible by the so-called dissociation of colors, — i. e. the juxtaposing of tints, the blending of which by the eye gives the desired color, without the loss of brightness which a mixing of pigments would involve. Thus by putting touches of black and white side by side, for instance, a gray results much brighter than could have been otherwise reached by mixing; or blue and red spots are blended by the eye to an extraordinarily vivid purple. Thus, by these methods, using the truth of color in the sense of following the nature of retinal functioning, Monet and his followers raised the color scale many degrees in brightness. Now we have seen that the eye loves light, warmth, strong color-effects, related to each other in the way that the eye must see them. Impressionism, as the name of the method just described, makes it more possible than it had been before to meet the demands of the eye for light and color, to recover "the innocence of the eye," in Ruskin's phrase. Truth to the local color of objects is relatively indifferent, unless that color is beautiful in itself; truth to the reciprocal relations and changes of hue is beauty, because it allows for the eye's own adaptations of its surroundings in the interest of its own functioning. Thus in this case, and to sum up, truth is synonymous with beauty, in so far as beauty is constituted by favorable stimulation of an organ. The further question, how far this vivid treatment of light is of importance for the realization of depth and distance, is not here entered on.

IV

The moment we touch upon line-form we are already, in strictness, beyond the elements. For with form enters the motor factor, which cannot be separated from the motor innervations of the whole body. It is possible, however, to abstract for the moment from the form as a unit, and to consider here only what may be called the quality of line. A line may be straight or broken, and if curved, curving continuously or brokenly, etc. That this quality of line is distinct from form may be shown by the simple experiment of turning a spiral — a logarithmic spiral, let us say — in differ-

ent ways about its focus. The æsthetic effect of the
figure is absolutely different in the different positions, and yet the feeling about the character of
the line itself seems to remain the same. In what
sense, and for what reasons, does this curved line
satisfy the demands of the eye? The discussion of
this question precipitates us at once into one of the
burning controversies of æsthetics, which may perhaps best be dealt with at this point.

An early answer to the question would have
been, that the eye is so hung in its muscles as to
move most easily in curved lines, and this easy
action in following the curve is felt as favorable
stimulation. But recent experiment [1] has shown
that the eye in fact moves by most irregular,
angular leaps from point to point of the figure.
The theory is therefore remodeled by substituting
for the movement sensations of the eye, the tendencies corresponding to those early movements
of touching imitative of the form, by which we
learned to know a form for what it is, and the
reproduction of feeling-tones belonging to the character of such movement. The movements of touching and feeling for a smooth continuous curved
object are themselves pleasant. This complex of
psychical factors makes a pleasurably stimulating
experience. The greater the tendency to complete
reproduction of these movements, that is, the
stronger the " bodily resonance," the more vivid

[1] G. M. Stratton, *Philos. Studien*, xx.

the pleasure. Whether we (with Groos) designate this as sympathetic reproduction, or (with Lipps) attribute to the figure the movements and the feelings which resound in us after this fashion, or even (with Witasek) insist on the purely ideal character of the reproduction, seems to me not essential to the explanation of the pleasing character of the experience, and hence of the beauty of the object. Not *that* we sympathetically reproduce ("Miterleben"), or "feel ourselves into" a form ("Einfühlen"), but *how* we do so, is the question.

All that Hogarth says of the beauty of the serpentine line, as "leading the eye a kind of chase," is fully in harmony with this view, if we add to the exploiting movements of the eye those other more important motor innervations of the body. But we should still have to ask, *what* kind of chase? Sharp, broken, starting lines might be the basis of a much more vivid experience, — but it would be æsthetically negative. "The complete sensuous experience of the spatial" is not enough, unless that experience is positively, that is, favorably toned. Clear or vivid seeing made possible by the form of the object is not enough. Only as *favorably* stimulating, that is, only as calling up ideal reproductions, or physical imitations, of movements which in themselves were suited to the functions of the organs involved, can forms be found positively æsthetic, that is, beautiful.

Moreover, we have to note here, and to emphasize,

that the organs involved are more than the eye, as has already been made plain. We cannot separate eye innervations from bodily innervations in general. And therefore " the demands of the eye " can never alone decide the question of the beauty of visual form. If it were not so, the favorable stimulation combined with repose of the eye would alone make the conditions of beauty. The " demands of the eye " must be interpreted as the demands of the eye plus the demands of the motor system, — the whole psychophysical personality, in short.

It is in these two principles,—" bodily resonance," and favorable as opposed to energetic functioning, — and these alone, that we have a complete refutation of the claim made by many artists to-day, that the phrase " demands of the eye" embodies a complete æsthetic theory. The sculptor Adolph Hildebrand, in his " Problem of Form in the Plastic Art " first set it forth as the task of the artist " to find a form which appears to have arisen only from the demands of the eye ; " [1] and this doctrine is to-day so widely held, that it must here be considered at some length.

It is the space-form, all that is seen, and not the object itself, that is the object of vision. Now in viewing a plastic object near at hand, the focus of the eye must be constantly changed between the nearer and further points. In a more distant view,

[1] *Das Problem der Form in d. bildenden Kunst*, 1897.

on the other hand (Hildebrand's " Fernbild "),
the contour is denoted by differences of light and
shadow, but it is nevertheless perceived in a single
act of accommodation. Moreover, being distant, the
muscles of accommodation are relaxed ; the eye
acts at rest. The " Fernbild " thus gives the only
unified picture of the three-dimensional complex,
and hence the only unity of space-values. In the
perception of this unity, the author holds, consists
the essential pleasure which the work of art gives
us. Hildebrand's treatment is difficult, and lends
itself to varying interpretations, which have laid
stress now on unity as the essential of art,[1] now on
" the joy in. the complete sensuous experience of
the spatial." [2] The latter seems in harmony with
the passage in which Hildebrand says " all pleasure in Form is pleasure in our not being obliged
to create this clearness for ourselves, in its being
created for us, nay, even forced upon us, by the
form itself."

But supposing the first interpretation correct :
supposing space-unity, conditioned by the unified
and reposeful act of seeing, to be the beauty we
seek — it is at once clear that the reduction of three
dimensions to two does not constitute unity even
for the eye alone ; how much less for the motor system of the whole body, which we have seen must be
involved. Hildebrand's " demands of the eye " re-

---

[1] A. Riehl, *Vierteljahrschr. f. wissensch. Philos.*, xxi, xxii.
[2] K. Groos, *Der Æsthetische Genuss*, 1902, p. 17.

solves itself into the stimulation plus repose of the ciliary muscle, — the organ of accommodation. A real unity even for the eye alone would have to include not only space relations in the third dimension, but relations of line and mass and color in the flat. As for the " complete sensuous experience of the spatial " (which would seem to be equivalent to Berenson's " tactile values "), the " clearness " of Hildebrand's sentence above quoted, it is evident that completeness of the experience does not necessarily involve the positive or pleasurable toning of the experience. The distinction is that between a beautiful and a completely realistic picture.

A further extension or restatement of this theory, in a recent article,[1] seems to me to express it in the most favorable way. Beauty is again connected with the functioning of our organs of perception (*Auffassungsorgane*). " We wish to be put into a fresh, lively, energetic and yet at the same time effortless activity. . . . The pleasure in form is a pleasure in this, that the conformation of the object makes possible or rather compels a natural purposeful functioning of our apprehending organs." But purposeful for what ? For visual form, evidently to the end of seeing clearly. The element of repose, of unity, hinted at in the " effortless " of the first sentence, disappears in the second. The

[1] Th. A. Meyer, " Das Formprinzip des Schönen," *Archiv. f. Phil.*, Bd. x.

organs of apprehension are evidently limited to the eye alone. It is not the perfect moment of stimulation and repose for the whole organism which is aimed at, but the complete sensuous experience of the spatial, again.

Hildebrand, to return to the more famous theorist, was writing primarily of sculpture, and would naturally confine himself to consideration of the plastic, which is an additional reason against making this interesting brochure, as some have done, the foundation of an æsthetics. It is rather the foundation of the sculptor's, perhaps even of the painter's technique, with reference to plastic elements alone. What it contains of universal significance, the demand for space-unity, based on the state of the eye in a union of rest and action, ignores all but one of the possible sources of rest and action for the eye, that of accommodation, and all the allied activities completely.

On the basis of the favorable stimulations of all these activities taken together, must we judge as pleasing the so-called quality of line. But it is clear that we cannot really separate the question of quality of line from that of form, figure, and arrangement in space. The motor innervations enter with the first, and the moment we have form at all, we have space-composition also. But space-composition means unity, and unity is the objective quality which must be translated, in our investigations, into æsthetic repose. It is thus with the study of composition that we pass from the study of the elements as favorably stimulating, to the study of the beauty of visual form.

V

We may begin by asking what, as a matter of fact, has been the arrangement of spaces to give æsthetic pleasure. The primitive art of all nations shows that it has taken the direction of symmetry about a vertical line. It might be said that this is the result of non-æsthetic influences, such as convenience of construction, technique, etc. [1] It is clear that much of the symmetry appearing in primitive art is due (1) to the conditions of construction, as in the form of dwellings, binding patterns, weaving and textile patterns generally; (2) to convenience in use, as in the shapes of spears, arrows, knives, two-handled baskets or jars; (3) to the imitation of animal forms, as in the shapes of pottery, etc. On the other hand, (1) a very great deal of symmetrical ornament maintains itself *against* the suggestions of the shape to which it is applied, as the ornaments of baskets, pottery, and all rounded objects; and (2) all distortion, disintegration, degradation of pattern-motives, often so marked as all but to destroy their meaning, is in the direction of geometrical symmetry. The early

[1] The following is adapted from the author's *Studies in Symmetry, Harvard Psychol. Studies*, vol. i, 1902.

art of all civilized nations shows the same characteristic. Now it might be said that, as there exists an instinctive tendency to imitate visual forms by motor impulses, the impulses suggested by the symmetrical form are in harmony with the system of energies of our bilateral organism, which is a system of double motor innervations, and thus fulfill our demand for a set of reactions corresponding to the organism as a whole. But we should then expect that all space arrangements which deviate from complete symmetry, and thus suggest motor impulses which do not correspond to the natural bilateral type, would fail to give æsthetic pleasure. Such, however, is not the case. Non-symmetrical arrangements of space are often extremely pleasing.

This contradiction disappears if we are able to show that the apparently non-symmetrical arrangement contains a hidden symmetry, and that all the elements of that arrangement contribute to bring about just that bilateral type of motor impulses which is characteristic of geometrical symmetry.

A series of experiments was arranged, in which one of two unequal lines of white on a black background being fixed in an upright position a certain distance from the centre, the other was shifted until the arrangement was felt to be pleasing. It was found that when two lines of different sizes were opposed, their relative positions corresponded to the relation of the arms of a balance, that is, a small line far from the centre was opposed

by a large one near the centre. A line pointing
out from the centre fitted this formula if taken
as "heavy," and pointing in, if taken as "light."
Similarly, objects of intrinsic interest and objects
suggesting depth in the third dimension were
"heavy" in the same interpretation. All this,
however, did not go beyond the proof that all
pleasing space-arrangements can be described in
terms of mechanical balance. But what was this
mechanical balance? A metaphor explains nothing,
and no one will maintain that the visual representation of a long line weighs more than a short one.
Moreover, the elements in the balance were so far
heterogeneous. The movement suggested by an
idea had been treated as if equivalent to the movement actually made by the eye in following a long
line; the intrinsic interest — that is, the ideal interest — of an object insignificant in form was
equated to the attractive power of a perspective,
which has, presumably, a merely physiological effect on the visual mechanism.

I believe, however, that the justification of this
apparent heterogeneity, and the basis for explanation, is given in the reduction of all elements to
their lowest term, — as objects for the expenditure
of attention. A large object and an "interesting"
object are "heavy" for the same reason, because
they call out the attention. And expenditure of
effort is expenditure of attention; thus, if an object on the outskirts of the field of vision requires

a wide sweep of the eye to take it in, it demands the expenditure of attention, and so is felt as "heavy." But what is "the expenditure of attention" in physiological terms? It is nothing more than the measure of the motor impulses directed to the object of attention. And whether the motor impulse appears as the tendency to fixate an object or as the tendency to follow out the suggestions of motion in the object, all reduces to the same physiological basis.

It may here be objected that our motor impulses are, nevertheless, still heterogeneous, inasmuch as some are toward the object of interest, and some along the line of movement. But it must be said, first, that these are not felt in the body, but transferred as values of weight to points in the picture, — it is the amount and not the direction of excitement that is counted; and secondly, that even if it were not so, the suggested movement along a line is felt as "weight" at a particular point.

From this point of view the justification of the metaphor of mechanical balance is quite clear. Given two lines, the most pleasing arrangement makes the larger nearer the centre, and the smaller far from it. This is balanced because the spontaneous impulse of attention to the near, large line equals in amount the involuntary expenditure of attention to apprehend the small, farther one.

We may thus think of a space to be composed

as a kind of target, in which certain spots or terri-
tories count more or less, both according to their
distance from the centre and according to what fills
them. Every element of a picture, in whatever way
it gains power to excite motor impulses, is felt as
expressing that power in the flat pattern. A noble
vista is understood and enjoyed as a vista, but it is
counted in the motor equation, our " balance," as a
spot of so much intrinsic value at such and such
a distance from the centre. The skillful artist will
fill his target in the way to give the maximum
of motor impulses with the perfection of balance
between them.

It is thus in a kind of substitutional symmetry,
or balance, that we have the objective condition or
counterpart of æsthetic repose, or unity. From this
point of view it is clearly seen in what respect the
unity of Hildebrand fails. He demands in the statue,
especially, but also in the picture, the flat surface
as a unity for the three dimensions. But it is only
with the flat space, won, if you will, by Hildebrand's
method, that the problem begins. Every point in
the third dimension counts, as has been said, in the
flat. The Fernbild is the beginning of beauty, but
within the Fernbild favorable stimulation and repose must still be sought. And repose or unity
is given by symmetry, subjectively the balance of
attention, inasmuch as this balance is a tension of
antagonistic impulses, an equilibrium, and thus an
inhibition of movement.

From this point of view, we are in a position to re-
fute Souriau's interesting analysis [1] of form as the
condition for the appreciation of content. He says
that form, in a picture for instance, has its value in
its power to produce (through its fixation and concentration of the eye) a mild hypnosis, in which,
as is well known, all suggestions come to us with
bewildering vividness. This is, then, just the state
in which the contents of the picture can most vividly impress themselves. Form, then, as the means
to content, by giving the conditions for suggestion, is
Souriau's account of it. In so far as form — in the
sense of unity — gives, through balance and equilibrium of impulses, the arrest of the personality, it
may indeed be compared with hypnotism. But this
arrest is not only a means, but an end in itself;
that æsthetic repose, which, as the unity of the
personality, is an essential element of the æsthetic
emotion as we have described it.

VI

There is no point of light or color, no contour, no
line, no depth, that does not contribute to the infinite complex which gives the maximum of experience
with the minimum of effort and which we call beauty
of form. But yet there is another way of viewing
the beautiful object, on which we touched in the
introduction to this chapter. So far, what we see is

[1] *La Suggestion en l'Art.*

only another name for *how* we see ; and the way of
seeing has proved to contain enough to bring to
stimulation and repose the psychophysical mechanism. But now we must ask, what relation has
meaning to beauty ? Is it an element, coördinate
with others, or something superposed ? or is it an
end in itself, the supreme end ? What relation to
the beauty of form has that quality of their works
by virtue of which Rembrandt is called a dreamer,
and Rodin a poet in stone ? What do we mean
when we speak of Sargent as a psychologist ? Is it
a virtue to be a poet in stone ? If it is, we must
somehow include in our concept of Beauty the
element of expression, by showing how it serves the
infinite complex. Or is it not an æsthetic virtue,
and Rodin is great artist and poet combined, and
not great artist because poet, as some would say ?
What is the relation of the objective content to
beauty of form ? In short, what place has the idea
in Beauty ?

In the preceding the place of separate objects
which have only an ideal importance has been made
clear. The gold-embroidered gauntlet in a picture counts as a patch of light, a trend of line, in a
certain spot ; but it counts more there, because it
is of interest for itself, and by thus counting more,
the idea has entered into the spatial balance, — the
idea has become itself form. Now it is the question
whether all "idea," which seems so heterogeneous
in its relation to form, does not undergo this trans-

mutation. It is at least of interest to see whether the facts can be so interpreted.

We have spoken of ideas as parts of an æsthetic whole. What of the idea of the whole? Corot used to say he painted a dream, and it is the dream of an autumn morning we see in his pictures. Millet portrays the sad majesty and sweetness of the life near the soil. How must we relate these facts to the views already won?

It has often been said that the view which makes the element of form for the eye alone, in the strictest sense, is erroneous, because there is no form for the eye alone. The very process of apprehending a line involves not only motor memories and impulses, but numberless ideal associations, and these associations constitute the line as truly as do the others. The impression of the line involves expression, a meaning which we cannot escape. The forms of things constitute a kind of dialect of life, — and thus it is that the theory of *Einfühlung* in its deepest sense is grounded. The Doric column causes in us, no doubt, motor impulses, but it means, and must mean, to us, the expression of internal energy through those very impulses it causes. " We ourselves are contracting our muscles, but we feel as if the lines were pulling and piercing, bending and lifting, pressing down and pushing up ; in short, as soon as the visual impression is really isolated, and all other ideas really excluded, then the motor impulses do not awake actions which are taken as actions of ourselves, but feelings of energy which are taken as energies of the visual forms and lines." [1] So the idea belonging to the object, and the psychophysical effect of the object are only obverse and inverse of the same phenomenon. And our pleasure in the form of the column is rather our appreciation of energy than our feeling of favorable stimulation. Admitting this reasoning, the meaning of a picture would be the same as its beauty, it is said. The heroic art of J.-F. Millet, for example, would be beautiful because it is the perfect expression of the simplicity and suffering of labor.

Let us examine this apparently reasonable theory. It is true that every visual element is understood as expression too. It is not true, however, that expression and impression are parallel and mutually corresponding beyond the elements. Suppose a concourse of columns covered by a roof, — the Parthenon. Those psychophysical changes induced by the sight now mutually check and modify each other. Can we say that there is a "meaning," like the energy of the column, corresponding to that complex? It is at least not energy itself. Ask the same as regards the lines and masses of a picture by Corot. In the sense in which we have taken "meaning," the only psychologically possible one, our reactions could be interpreted only by some mood. If the column means energy because it makes us tower, then the picture must mean what

[1] H. Münsterberg, *The Principles of Art Education*, p. 87.

it makes us do. That is, a combination of feathery fronds and horizontal lines of water, bathed in a gray-green silvery mist, can "mean" only a repose lightened by a grave yet cheerful spirit. In short, this theory of expressiveness cannot go beyond the mood or moral quality. In the sense of *information*, the theory of *Einfühlung* contributes nothing. Now, in this limited sense, we have indeed no reason to contradict it, but simply to point out that it holds only in this extremely limited sense. When we see broad sweeping lines we interpret them by sympathetic reproduction as strength, energy. When those sweeping lines are made part of a Titan's frame, we get the same effect plus the associations which belong to distinctively muscular energy. Those same lines might define the sweep of a drapery, or the curve of an infant's limbs. Now all that part of the meaning which belongs to the lines themselves remains constant under whatever circumstances ; and it is quite true that a certain feeling-tone, a certain moral quality, as it were, belongs, say, to Raphael's pictures, in which this kind of outline is to be found. But as belonging to a Titan, the additional elements of understanding are not due to sympathetic reproduction. They are not parallel with the motor suggestions ; they are simply an associational addition, due to our information about the power of men with muscles like that. That there are secondary motor elements as a reverberation of these ideal elements need not be denied. But they are not directly due to the form. Now such part of our response to a picture as is directly induced by the form, we have a right to include in the æsthetic experience. It will, however, in every work of art of even the least complexity, be expressible only as a mood, very indefinite, often indescribable. To make this "meaning," then, the essential aim of a picture seems unreasonable.

It is evident that in experience we do not, as a matter of fact, separate the mood which is due to sympathy from the ideal content of the picture. Corot paints a summer dawn. We cannot separate our pleasure in the sight from our pleasure in the understanding; yet it is the visual complex that gives us the mood, and the meaning of the scene is due to factors of association. The " serene and happy dream," the " conviction of a solemn and radiant Arcadia," are not " expression " in that inevitable sense in which we agreed to take it, but the result of a most extended upbuilding of ideal (that is, associational) elements.

The "idea," then, as we have propounded it, is not, as was thought possible, an integral and essential part, but an addition to the visual form, and we have still to ask what is its value. But in so far as it is an addition, its effect may be in conflict with what we may call the feeling-tone produced by sympathetic reproduction. In that case, one must yield to the other. Now it is not probable that even the most convinced adherents of the expression theory would hold that if expression or beauty *must* go, expression should be kept. They only say that expression *is* beauty. But the moment it is admitted that there is a beauty of form independent of the ideal element, this theory can no longer stand. If there is a conflict, the palm must be given to the direct, rather than the indirect, factor. Indeed, when there is such a conflict, the primacy must always be with the medium suited to the organ, the sensuous factor. For if it were not so, and expression *were* beauty, then that would have to be most beautiful which was most expressive. And even if we disregard the extraordinary conclusions to which this would lead, — the story pictures preferred to those without a story, the photographic reproductions preferred to the symphonies of color and form,—we should be obliged to admit something still more incendiary. Expression is always of an ideal content, is of something to express; and it is unquestioned that in words, and in words alone, can we get nearest to the inexpressible. Then literature, as being the most expressive, would be the highest art, and we should be confronted with a hierarchy of arts, from that down.

Now, in truth, the real lover of beauty knows that no one art is superior to another. "Each in his separate star," they reign alone. In order to be equal, they must depend on their material, not on that common quality of imaginative thought which each has in a differing degree, and all less than literature.

The idea, we conclude, is then indeed subordinate, — a by-product, unless by chance it can enter into, melt into, the form. This case we have clearest in the example, already referred to, of the gold-embroidered gauntlet, or the jeweled chalice, — say the Holy Grail in Abbey's pictures, — which counts more or less, in the spatial balance, according to its intrinsic interest.

We have seen that through sympathetic reproduction a certain mood is produced, which becomes a kind of emotional envelope for the picture, — a favorable stimulation of the whole, a raising of the whole harmony one tone, as it were. Now the further ideal content of the picture may so closely belong to this basis that it helps it along. Thus all that we know about dawn — not only of a summer morning — helps us to see, and seeing to rejoice, in Corot's silvery mist or Monet's iridescent shimmers. All that we know and feel about the patient majesty of labor in the fields, next the earth, helps us to get the slow, large rhythm, the rich gloom of Millet's pictures. But it is the rhythm and the gloom that are the beauty, and the idea reinforces our consciousness thereof. The idea is a sounding-board for the beauty, and so can be truly said to enter into the form.

But there are still some lions in the path of our theory. The greatest of modern sculptors is reputed to have reached his present altitude by the passionate pursuance of Nature, and of the expressions of Nature. And few can see Rodin's work without being at once in the grip of the emotion or fact he has chosen to depict. A great deal of contemporary criticism on modern tendencies in art rests on the intention of expression, and expression alone, attributed to him. It is said of him: " The solicitude for ardent expression overmasters every æsthetic consideration. . . . He is a poet with stone as his instrument of expression. He makes it express emotions that are never found save in music or in psychological and lyric literature." [1]

Now while the last is undoubtedly true, I believe that the first is not only not true, but that it is proved to be so by Rodin's own procedure and utterances, and that, if we understand his case aright, it is for beauty alone that he lives. He has related his search for the secret of Michael Angelo's design, and how he found it in the rhythm of two planes rather than four, the Greek composition. This system of tormented form is one way of referring the body to the geometry of an imagined rectangular block inclosing the whole.

[2] " The ordinary Greek composition of the body,

[1] C. Mauclair, " The Decorative Sculpture of August Rodin," *International Monthly*, vol. iii.

[2] D. S. MacColl, *Nineteenth Century Art*, 1902, p. 101.

he puts it, depends on a rhythm of four lines, four volumes, four planes. If the line of the shoulders and pectorals slopes from right to left (the man resting on his right leg) the line across the hips takes the reverse slope, and is followed by that of the knees, while the line of the first echoes that of the shoulders. Thus we get the rhythm A B B A, and the balancing volumes set up a corresponding play of planes. Michael Angelo so turns the body on itself that he reduces the four to two big planes, one facing, the other swept round to the side of the block." That is, he gets geometrical enveloping lines for his design. And, in fact, there is no sculpture which is more wonderful in design than Rodin's. I quote Mr. MacColl again. " It has been said that the ' Bourgeois de Calais ' is a group of single figures, possessing no unity of design, or at best affording only a single point of view. Those who say so have never examined it with attention. The way in which these figures move among themselves, as the spectator walks round, so as to produce from every fresh angle sweeping commanding lines, each of them thus playing a dozen parts at once, is surely one of the most astounding feats of the genius of design. Nothing in the history of art is exactly comparable with it."

In short, it is the design, for all his words, that Rodin cares for. He calls it Nature, because he sees, and can see Nature only that way. But as he said to some one who suggested that there might be a danger in too close devotion to Nature, "Yes, for a mediocre artist!" It is for the sake of the strange new beauty, "the unedited poses," "the odd beautiful huddle [1] of lines," in a stooping or squatting form, that all these wild and subtle moments are portrayed. The limbs must be adjusted or surprised in some pattern beyond their own. The ideas are the occasion and the excuse for new outlines, — that is all.

This is all scarcely less true of Millet, whom we have known above all as the painter who has shown the simple common lot of labor as divine. But he, too, is artist for the sake of beauty first. He sees two peasant women, one laden with grass, the other with fagots. "From far off, they are superb, they balance their shoulders under the weight of fatigue, the twilight swallows their forms. It is beautiful, it is great as a mystery." [2]

The idea is, as I said, from this point of view, a means to new beauty; and the stranger and subtler the idea, the more original the forms. The more unrestrained the expression of emotion in the figures, the more chance to surprise them in some new lovely pattern. It is thus, I believe, that we may interpret the seeming trend of modern sculpture, and so much, indeed, of all modern art, to the "expressive beauty" path. "The mediocre artist" will lose beauty in seeking expression, the great

---

[1] Said of Degas. MacColl.
[2] Sensier, *Vie et Œuvre de J.-F. Millet.*

artist will pursue his idea for the sake of the new beauty it will yield.

Thus it seems that the stumbling blocks in the way of our theory are not insurmountable after all. From every point of view, it is seen to be possible to transmute the idea into a helpmeet to the form. Visual beauty is first beauty to the eye and to the frame, and the mind cherishes and enriches this beauty with all its own stored treasures. The stimulation and repose of the psychophysical organism alone can make one thrill to visual form ; but the thrill is deeper and more satisfying if it engage the whole man, and be reinforced from all the sources.

VII

But we ought to note a borderland in which the concern is professedly not with beauty, but with ideas of life. Aristotle's lover of knowledge, who rejoiced to say of a picture " This is that man," is the inspirer of drawing as opposed to the art of visual form.

It is not beauty we seek from the Rembrandt and Dürer of the etchings and woodcuts, from Hogarth, Goya, Klinger, down to Leech and Keene and Du Maurier ; it is not beauty, but ideas, — information, irony, satire, life-philosophy. Where there is a conflict, beauty, as we have defined it, goes to the wall. We may trace, perhaps, the ground of this in the highly increased amount of symbolic, associative power given, and required, in the black and white. Even to understand such a picture demands such an enormous amount of unconscious mental supplementation that it is natural to find the æsthetic centre of gravity in that element.

The first conditions of the work, that is, determine its trend and aim. The part played by imagination in our vision of an etching is and must be so important, that it is, after all, the imaginative part which outweighs the given. Nor do we desire the given to infringe upon the ideal field. Thus do we understand that for most drawings a background vague and formless is the desideratum. " Such a tone is the foil for psychological moments, as they are handled by Goya, for instance, with barbarically magnificent nakedness. On a background which is scarcely indicated, with few strokes, which barely suggest space, he impales like a butterfly the human type, mostly in a moment of folly or wickedness. . . . The least definition of surrounding would blunt his (the artist's) keenness, and make his vehemence absurd." [1]

This theory of the aim of black and white is confirmed by the fact that while a painting is composed for the size in which it is painted, and becomes another picture if reproduced in another measure, the size of drawings is relatively indifferent ; reduced or enlarged, the effect is approxi-

[1] Max Klinger, *Malerei u. Zeichnung*, 1903, p. 42.

mately the same, because what is given to the eye is such a small proportion of the whole experience. The picture is only the cue for a complete structure of ideas.

Here is a true case of *Anders-streben*, that " partial alienation from its own limitations, by which the arts are able, not indeed to supply the place of each other, but reciprocally to lend each other new forces." [1] It is by its success as representation that the art of the burin and needle — Griffelkunst, as Klinger names it — ought first to be judged. This is not saying that it may not also possess beauty of form to a high degree, — only that this beauty of form is not its characteristic excellence.

In what consists the beauty of visual form? If this question could be answered in a sentence our whole discussion of the abstract formula for beauty would have been unnecessary. But since we know what the elements of visual form must do to bring about the æsthetic experience, it has been the aim of the preceding pages to show how those elements must be determined and related. The eye, the psychophysical organism, must be favorably stimulated; these, and such colors, combinations, lines as we have described, are fitted to do it. It must be brought to repose; these, and such relations between lines and colors as we have set forth, are fitted to do it, for reasons we have given. It is to the eye and all that waits upon it that the first and

[1] W. Pater, *The Renaissance: Essay on Giorgione.*

the last appeal of fine art must be made; and in so far as the emotion or the idea belonging to a picture or a statue waits upon the eye, in so far does it enter into the characteristic excellence, that is, the beauty of visual form.

B. SPACE COMPOSITION AMONG THE OLD MASTERS

I

THE preceding pages have set forth the concrete facts of visible beauty, and the explanation of our feelings about it. It is also interesting, however, to see how these principles are illustrated and confirmed in the masterpieces of art. A statistical study, undertaken some years ago with the purpose of dealing thus with the hypothesis of substitutional symmetry in pictorial composition, has given abundance of material, which I shall set forth, at otherwise disproportionate length, as to a certain extent illustrative of the methods of such study. It is clear that this is but one of many possible investigations in which the preceding psychological theories may be further illuminated. The text confines itself to pictures; but the functions of the elements of visual form are valid as well for all visual art destined to fill a bounded area. The discussion will then be seen to be only ostensibly limited in its reference. For picture might always be read space arrangement within a frame.

In the original experimental study of space arrangements, the results of which were given at length on page 111, the elements of form in a picture were reduced to *size* or *mass*, *depth* in the third dimension, *direction*, and *interest*. Direction was further analyzed into direction of *motion* or *attention* (of persons or objects in the picture), an ideal element, that is; and direction of *line*. For the statistical study, a given picture was then divided in half by an imaginary vertical line, and the elements appearing on each side of this line were set off against each other to see how far they lent themselves to description by substitutional symmetry. Thus: in B. van der Helst's "Portrait of Paul Potter," the head of the subject is entirely to left of the central line, as also his full face and frontward glance. His easel is right, his body turned sharply to right, and both hands, one holding palette and brushes, are stretched down to right. Thus the greater mass is to the left, and the general direction of line is to the right; elements of interest in the head, left; in implements, right. This may be schematized in the equation $(Lt.)\ M. + I. = (Rt.)\ I. + L.$

Pieter de Hooch, "The Card-Players," in Buckingham Palace, portrays a group completely on the right of the central line, all facing in to the table between them. Directly behind them is a high light window, screened, and high on the wall to the extreme right are a picture and hanging cloaks. All goes to emphasize the height, mass, and interest of the right side. On the left, which is otherwise empty, is a door half the height of the window, giving on a brightly lighted courtyard, from which is entering a woman, also in light clothing. The light streams in diagonally across the floor. Thus, with all the " weight " on the right, the effect of this deep vista on the left and of its brightness is to give a complete balance, while the suggestion of line from doorway and light makes, together with the central figure, a roughly outlined V, which serves to bind together all the elements. Equation, (Lt.) V. + I. = (Rt.) M. + I.

The thousand pictures on which the study was based[1] were classified for convenience into groups, — Religious, Portrait, Genre, and Landscape. It was found on analysis that the functions of the elements came out clearly, somewhat as follows.

Of the religious pictures, only the " Madonnas Enthroned " and other altar-pieces are considered at this point as presenting a simple type, in which it is easy to show the variations from symmetry. In all these pictures the balance comes in between the interest in the Infant Christ, sometimes together with direction of attention to him, on one side, and other elements on the other. When the first side

[1] One thousand reproductions of old masters from F. Bruckmann's *Classischer Bilderschatz*, Munich, omitting frescoes and pictures of which less than the whole was given.

is especially " heavy " the number of opposing elements increases, and especially takes the form of vista and line, which have been experimentally found to be powerful in attracting attention. Where there are no surrounding worshipers, we notice remarkable frequency in the use of vista and line, and, in general, balance is brought about through the disposition of form rather than of interests. The reason for this would appear to be that the lack of accessories in the persons of saints, worshipers, etc., and the consequent increase in the size of Madonna and Child in the picture, heightens the effect of any given outline, and so makes the variations from symmetry greater. This being the case, the compensations would be stronger; and as we have learned that vista and line are of this character, we see why they are needed.

The portrait class is an especially interesting object for study, inasmuch as while its general type is very simple and constant, for this very reason the slightest variations are sharply felt, and have their very strongest characteristic effect. The general type of the portrait composition is, of course, the triangle with the head at the apex, and this point is also generally in the central line; nevertheless, great richness of effect is brought about by emphasizing variations. For instance, the body and head are, in the great majority of cases, turned in the same way, giving the strongest possible emphasis to the direction of attention, — especially

powerful, of course, where all the interest is in the
personality. But it is to be observed that the very
strongest suggestion of direction is given by the
direction of the glance; and in no case, when most
of the other elements are directed in one way, does
the glance fail to come backward. With the head
on one side of the central line, of course the greatest
interest is removed to one side, and the element of
direction is brought in to balance. Again, with this
decrease in symmetry, we see a significant increase
in the use of the especially effective elements, vista
and line. In fact, the use of the small deep vista is
almost confined to the class with heads not in the
middle. The direction of the glance also plays an
important part. Very often the direction of movement alone is not sufficient to balance the powerful
M. + I. of the other side, and the eye has to be
attracted by a definite object of interest. This is
usually the hand, with or without an implement,
— like the palette, etc., of our first examples, — or
a jewel, vase, or bit of embroidery. This is very
characteristic of the portraits of Rembrandt and
Van Dyck.

In general, it may be said that (1) portraits
with the head in the centre of the frame show a
balance between the direction of suggested movement on one side, and mass or direction of attention,
or both together, on the other; while (2) portraits
with the head not in the centre show a balance between mass and interest on one side, and direction

of attention, or of line, or vista, or combinations of these, on the other.

Still more unsymmetrical in their framework than portraits, in fact the most unfettered type of all, are the genre pictures. As these are pictures with a human interest, and full of action and particular points of interest, it was to be expected that interest would be the element most frequently appearing. In compositions showing great variations from geometrical symmetry, it was also to be expected that vista and line, elements which have been noted comparatively seldom up to this point, should suddenly appear strongly; for, as being the most strikingly " heavy " of the elements, they serve to compensate for other variations combined.

The landscape is another type of unfettered composition. It was of course to be expected that in pictures without action there should be little suggestion of attention or of direction of movement. But the most remarkable point is the presence of vista in practically every example. It is, of course, natural that somewhere in almost every picture there should be a break to show the horizon line, for the sake of variety, if for nothing else ; but what is significant is the part played by this break in the balancing of the picture. In about two thirds of the examples the vista is inclosed by lines, or masses, and when near the centre, as being at the same time the "heaviest" part of the picture, it serves as a fulcrum or centre to bind the parts —

always harder to bring together than in the other types of pictures — into a close unity. The most frequent form of this arrangement is a diagonal, which just saves itself by turning up at its far end. Thus the mass, and hence usually the special interest of the picture, is on the one side, on the other the vista and the sloping line of the diagonal. In very few cases is the vista behind an attractive or noticeable part of the picture, the fact showing that it acts in opposition to the latter, leading the eye away from it, and thus serving at once the variety and richness of the picture, and its unity. A complete diagonal would have line and vista both working at the extreme outer edge of the picture, and thus too strongly, — unless, indeed, balanced by very striking elements near the other edge.

This function of the vista as a unifying element is of interest in connection with the theory of Hildebrand, [1] that the landscape should have a narrow foreground and wide background, since that is most in conformity with our experience. He adduces Titian's "Sacred and Profane Love" as an example. But of the general principle it may be said that not the reproduction of nature, but the production of beauty, is the aim of composition, and that this aim is best reached by focusing the eye by a narrow background, i. e. vista. No matter how much it wanders, it returns to that central spot and is held there, keeping hold on all the other elements.

[1] *Op. cit.*, p. 55.

Of Hildebrand's example it may be said that the pyramidal composition, with the dark and tall tree in the centre, effectually accomplishes the binding together of the two figures, so that a vista is not needed. A wide background without that tree would leave them rather disjointed.

In general, it may be said that balance in landscape is effected between mass and interest on one side and vista and line on the other; and that union is given especially by the use of vista.

II

The experimental treatment of the isolated elements detected the particular function of each in distributing attention in the field of view. But while all are possibly operative in a given picture, some are given, as we have seen, much more importance than others, and in pictures of different types different elements predominate. In those classes with a general symmetrical framework, such as the altar and Madonna pieces, the elements of interest and direction of attention determine the balance, for they appear as variations in a symmetry which has already, so to speak, disposed of mass and line. They give what action there is, and where they are very strongly operative, they are opposed by salient lines and deep vistas, which act more strongly on the attention than does mass. Interest keeps its predominance throughout the types, except in the portraits, where the head is usually in the central line. But even among the portraits it has a respectable representation, as jewels, embroideries, beautiful hands, etc., count largely too in composition.

The direction of attention is most operative among the portraits. Since these pictures represent no action, it must be given by those elements which move and distribute the attention; in accordance with which principle we find line also unusually influential. As remarked above, altar-pieces and Madonna pictures, also largely without action, depend largely for it on the direction of attention.

The vista, as said above, rivets and confines the attention. We can, therefore, understand how it is that in the genre pictures it appears very numerous. The active character of these pictures naturally requires to be modified, and the vista introduces a powerful balancing element, which is yet quiet; or, it might be said, inasmuch as energy is certainly expended in plunging down the third dimension, the vista introduces an element of action of counterbalancing character. In the landscape it introduces the principal element of variety. It is always to be found in those parts of the picture which are opposed to other powerful elements, and the "heavier" the other side, the deeper the vista. Also in pictures with two groups it serves as a kind of fulcrum, or unifying element, inasmuch as it rivets the attention between the two detached sides.

The direction of suggestion by means of the indication of a line, quite naturally is more frequent in the Madonna picture and portrait classes. Both these types are of large simple outline, so that line would be expected to tell. In a decided majority of cases, combined with vista — the shape being more or less a diagonal slope — it is clear that it acts as a kind of bond between the two sides, carrying the attention without a break from one to the other.

The element of mass requires less comment. It appears in greatest number in those pictures which have little action, i. e. portraits and landscapes, and which are yet not symmetrical, — in which last case mass is, of course, already balanced. In fact, it must of necessity exert a certain influence in every unsymmetrical picture, and so its percentage, even for genre pictures, is large.

Thus we may regard the elements as both attracting attention to a certain spot and dispersing it over a field. Those types which are of a static character (landscapes, altar-pieces) abound in elements which disperse the attention; those which are of a dynamic character (genre pictures), in those which make it stable. The ideal composition seems to combine the dynamic and static elements, — to animate, in short, the whole field of view, but in a generally bilateral fashion. The elements, in substitutional symmetry, are then simply means of introducing variety and action. As a dance in which there are complicated steps gives the actor and beholder a varied and thus vivified "balance," and is thus more beautiful than the simple walk, so a picture composed in substitutional symmetry is more rich in its suggestions of motor impulse, and thus more beautiful, than an example of geometrical symmetry.

III

The particular functions of the elements which are substituted for geometrical symmetry have been made clear; their presence lends variety and richness to the balance of motor impulses. But this quality of repose, or unity, given by balance, is also enriched by a unity for intuition, — a large outline in which all the elements are held together. Now this way of holding together varies; and I believe that it bears a very close relation to the subject and purpose of the picture.

Examples of these types of composition may best be found by analyzing a few well-known pictures. We may begin with the class first studied, the Altar-piece, choosing a picture by Botticelli, in the Florence Academy. Under an arch is draped a canopy held up by angels; under this, again, sits the Madonna with the Child on her lap, on a throne, at the foot of which, on each side, stand three saints. The outline of the whole is markedly pyramidal; in fact, there are, broadly speaking, three pyramids, — of the arch, the canopy, and the grouping. A second, much less symmetrical example of this type, is given by another Botticelli in the Academy, — "Spring." Here the central female figure, topped by the floating Cupid, is slightly raised above the others, which, however, bend slightly inward, so that a triangle, or pyramid with very obtuse angle at the apex, is suggested; and the whole, which at first glance seems a little scattered, is at once felt, when this is grasped, as closely bound together.

Closely allied to this is the type of the Holbein "Madonna of Burgomaster Meyer," in the Grand Ducal Castle, Darmstadt. It is true that the same pyramid is given by the head of the Madonna against the shell-like background, and her spreading cloak which envelops the kneeling donors. But still more salient is the diamond form given by the descending rows of these worshiping figures, especially against the dark background of the Madonna's dress. A second example, without the pyramid backing, is found in Rubens's "Rape of the Daughters of Leucippus," in the Alte Pinakothek at Munich. Here the diamond shape formed by the horses and struggling figures is most remarkable, — an effect of lightness which will be discussed later in interpreting the types.

A third type, the diagonal, is given in an "Evening Landscape" by Cuyp, in the Buckingham

Palace, London. High trees and cliffs, horsemen and others, occupy one side, and the mountains in the background, the ground and the clouds, all slope gradually down to the other side.

It is a natural transition from this type to the V-shape of the landscapes by Aart van der Neer, " Dutch Villages," in the London National Gallery and in the Rudolphinum at Prague, respectively. Here are trees and houses on each side, gradually sloping to the centre to show an open sky and deep vista. Other examples, of course, show the opening not exactly in the centre.

In the " Concert " by Giorgione, in the Pitti Gallery, Florence, is seen the less frequent type of the square. The three figures turned toward each other with heads on the same level make almost a square space-shape, although it might be said that the central player gives a pyramidal foundation. This last may also be said of Verrocchio's " Tobias and the Archangels " in the Florence Academy, for the square, or other rectangle, is again lengthened by the pyramidal shape of the two central figures. The unrelieved square, it may here be interpolated, is not often found except in somewhat primitive examples. Still less often observed is the oval type of " Samson's Wedding Feast," Rembrandt, in the Royal Gallery, Dresden. Here one might, by pressing the interpretation, see an obtuse-angled double-pyramid with the figure of Delilah for an apex, but a few very irregular pictures seem to fall best under the given classification.

Last of all, it must be remarked that the great majority of pictures show a combination of two or even three types; but these are usually subordinated to one dominant type. Such, for instance, is the case with many portraits, which are markedly pyramidal, with the double-pyramid suggested by the position of the arms, and the inverted pyramid, or V, in the landscape background. The diagonal sometimes just passes over into the V-shape, or into the pyramid; or the square is combined with both.

What types are characteristic of the different kinds of pictures? In order to answer this question we must ask first, What are the different kinds of pictures? One answer, at least, is at once suggested to the student on a comparison of the pictures with their groupings according to subjects. All those which represent the Madonna enthroned, with all variations, with or without saints, shepherds, or Holy Family, are very quiet in their action; that is, it is not really an action at all which they represent, but an attitude, — the attitude of contemplation. This is no less true of the pictures we may call " Adorations," in which, indeed, the contemplative attitude is still more marked. On the other hand, such pictures as the " Descents," the " Annunciations," and very many of the miscellaneous religious, allegorical, and genre pictures, portray a definite action or event. Now the pyramid type is characteristic of the "contemplative" pictures in a much higher degree. A class which might be supposed to suggest the same treatment in composition is that of the portraits, — absolute lack of action being the rule. And we find, indeed, that no single type is represented within it except the pyramid and double-pyramid, with eighty-six per cent. of the former. Thus it is evident that for the type of picture which expresses the highest degree of quietude, contemplation, concentration, the pyramid is the characteristic type of composition. Among the so-called "active" pictures, the diagonal and V-shaped types are most numerous.

The landscape picture presents a somewhat different problem. It cannot be described as either "active" or "passive," inasmuch as it does not express either an attitude or an event. There is no definite idea to be set forth, no point of concentration, as with the altar-pieces and the portraits, for instance; and yet a unity is demanded. An examination of the proportions of the types shows at once the characteristic type to be here also the diagonal and V-shaped.

It is now necessary to ask what must be the interpretation of the use of these types of composition. Must we consider the pyramid the expression of passivity, the diagonal or V-shape, of activity? But the greatly predominating use of the second for landscapes would remain unexplained, for at least nothing can be more reposeful than the latter. It may aid the solution of the problem to remember that the composition taken as a whole has to meet the demand for unity, at the same time that it allows free play to the natural expression of the subject. The altar-piece has to bring about a concentration of attention to express or induce a feeling of reverence. This is evidently accomplished by the suggestion of the converging lines to the fixation of the high point in the picture, — the small area occupied by the Madonna and Child, — and by the subordination of the free play of other elements. The contrast between the broad base and the apex gives a feeling of solidity, of repose ; and it seems not unreasonable to suppose that the tendency to rest the eyes above the centre of the picture directly induces the associated mood of reverence or worship. Thus the pyramidal form serves two ends ; primarily that of giving unity, and secondarily, by the peculiarity of its shape, that of inducing the feeling-tone appropriate to the subject of the picture.

Applying this principle to the so-called " active " pictures, we see that the natural movement of attention between the different " actors " in the picture must be allowed for, while yet unity is secured. And it is clear that the diagonal type is just fitted for this. The attention sweeps down from the high side to the low, from which it returns through some backward suggestion of lines or interest in the objects of the high side. Action and reaction — move-

ment and return of attention — is inevitable under
the conditions of this type; and this it is which
allows the free play, — which, indeed, *constitutes*
and expresses the activity belonging to the subject,
just as the fixation of the pyramid constitutes the
quietude of the religious picture. Thus it is that
the diagonal composition is particularly suited to
portray scenes of grandeur, and to induce a feeling
of awe in the spectator, because only here can the
eye rove in one large sweep from side to side of the
picture, recalled by the mass and interest of the side
from which it moves. The swing of the pendulum
is here widest, so to speak, and all the feeling-tones
which belong to wide, free movement are called into
play. If, at the same time, the element of the deep
vista is introduced, we have the extreme of concentration combined with the extreme of movement;
and the result is a picture in the "grand style"
— comparable to high tragedy — in which all the
feeling-tones which wait on motor impulses are, as
it were, while yet in the same reciprocal relation,
tuned to the highest pitch. Such a picture is
the " Finding of the Ring," Paris Bordone, in the
Venice Academy. All the mass and the interest
and the suggestion of attention is toward the right,
the sweep of the downward lines and of the magnificent perspective toward the left, and the effect
of the whole space composition is of superb largeness of life and feeling. Compare Titian's " Presentation of the Virgin," also the two great composi-

tions by Veronese, "Martyrdom of St. Mark," etc., in the Doge's Palace, Venice, and "Esther before Ahasuerus," in the Uffizi, Florence. In these last two, the mass, direction of interest, movement, and attention are toward the left, while all the lines tend diagonally to the right, where a vista is also suggested, — the diagonal making a V just at the end. Here, too, the effect is of magnificence and vigor.

If, then, the pyramid belongs to contemplation, the diagonal to action, what can be said of landscape? It is without action, it is true, and yet does not express that positive quality, that *will* not to act, of the rapt contemplation. The landscape uncomposed is negative, and it demands unity. Its type of composition, then, must give it something positive besides unity. It lacks both concentration and action; but it can gain them both from a space composition which shall combine unity with a tendency to movement. And this is given by the diagonal and V-shaped type. This type merely allows free play to the natural tendency of the "active" picture; but it constrains the neutral, inanimate landscape. The shape itself imparts motion to the picture : the sweep of line, the concentration of the vista, the unifying power of the inverted triangle between two masses, act, as it were, externally to the suggestion of the object itself. There is always enough quiet in a landscape, — the overwhelming suggestion of the horizontal suffices for that ; it is movement that is needed for richness of effect, and, as I have shown, no type imparts the feeling of movement so strongly as the diagonal and V-shaped type of composition. Landscapes need energy to produce "stimulation," not repression, and so the diagonal type is proportionately more numerous.

The rigid square is found only at an early stage in the development of composition. Moreover, all the examples are "story" pictures, for the most part scenes from the lives of the saints, etc. Many of them are double-centre, — square, that is, with a slight break in the middle, the grouping purely logical, to bring out the relations of the characters. Thus, in the "Dream of Saint Martin," Simone Martini, a fresco at Assisi, the saint lies straight across the picture with his head in one corner. Behind him on one side stand the Christ and angels, grouped closely together, their heads on the same level. These are all, of course, in one sense symmetrical, — in the weight of interest, at least, — but they are completely amorphous from an æsthetic point of view. The forms, that is, do not count at all, — only the meanings. The story is told by a clear separation of the parts, and as, in most stories, there are two principal actors, it merely happens that they fall into the two sides of the picture. On the other hand, a rigid geometrical symmetry is also characteristic of early composition, and these two facts seem to contradict each other. But it is to be noted, first, that the rigid geometrical symmetry belongs only to the "Madonna Enthroned," and general "Adoration" pieces; and secondly, that this very rigidity of symmetry in details can coexist with variations which destroy balance. Thus, in a "Madonna Enthroned" of Giotto, where absolute symmetry in detail is kept, the Child sits far out on the right knee of the Madonna.

It would seem that the symmetry of these early pictures was not dictated by a conscious demand for symmetrical arrangement, or rather for real balance, else such failures would hardly occur. The presence of geometrical symmetry is more easily explained as the product, in large part, of technical conditions: of the fact that these pictures were painted as altar-pieces to fill a space definitely symmetrical in character — often, indeed, with architectural elements intruding into it. We may even connect the Madonna pictures with the temple images of the classic period, to explain why it was natural to paint the object of worship seated exactly facing the worshiper. Thus we may separate the two classes of pictures, the one giving an object of worship, and thus taking naturally, as has been said, the pyramidal, symmetrical shape, and being moulded to symmetry by all other suggestions of technique ; the other aiming at nothing except logical clearness. This antithesis of the symbol and the story has a most interesting parallel in the two great classes of primitive art — the one symbolic, merely suggestive, shaped by the space it had to fill, and so degenerating into the slavishly symmetrical; the other descriptive, "story-telling," and without a trace of space composition. On neither side is there evidence of direct æsthetic feeling. Only in the course of artistic development do we find the rigid, yet often unbalanced, symmetry relaxing into a free substitutional symmetry, and the formless narrative crystallizing into a really unified and balanced space-form. The two antitheses approach each other in the "balance" of the masterpieces of civilized art — in which, for the first time, a real feeling for space composition makes itself felt.

V

THE BEAUTY OF MUSIC

V

THE BEAUTY OF MUSIC

I

THERE is a story, in Max Müller's amusing reminiscences, of how Mendelssohn and David once played, in his hearing, Beethoven's later sonatas for piano and violin, and of how they shrugged their shoulders, and opined the old man had not been quite himself when he wrote them. In the history of music it seems to be a rule almost without exceptions, that the works of genius are greeted with contumely. The same is no doubt true, though to a much less degree, of other arts, but in music it seems that the critics proposed also excellent reasons for their vehemence. And it is instructive to observe that the objections, and the reasons for the objections, recur, after the original object of wrath has passed into acceptance, nay, into dominance of the musical world. One may also descry one basic controversy running through all these utterances, even when not explicitly set forth.

It was made a reproach to Beethoven, as it has been made a reproach to Richard Strauss, that he sacrificed the beauty of form to expression; and it

was rejoined, perhaps less in the old time than
now, that expression was itself the end and meaning of music. Now the works of genius, as we
have seen, after all take care of themselves. But
it is of greatest significance for the theory of
music, as of all art, that in the circle of the years,
the same contrasting views, grown to ever sharper
opposition, still greet the appearance of new work.
It was with Wagner, as all the world knows, that
the question came first to complete formulation.
His invention of the music-drama rested on his famous theory of music as the heightened medium of
expression, glorified speech, which accordingly demands freedom to follow all the varying *nuances*
of feeling and emotion. Music has always been
called the language of the emotions, but Wagner
based his views not only on the popular notion, but
on the metaphysical theories of Schopenhauer; in
particular, on the view that music is the objectification of the will. Herbert Spencer followed with
the thesis that music has its essential source in
the cadences of emotional speech. In opposition
primarily to Wagner, the so-called formalists were
represented by Hanslick, who wrote his well-known
·· The Beautiful in Music " to show that though
music has a limited capacity of expression, its aim
is formal or logical perfection alone. The expres-
sionist school could not contradict the undoubted
fact that chords and intervals which are harmonious show certain definite physical and mathemati-

cal relationships, that, in other words, our musical preferences appear to be closely related to, if not determined by, these relationships. Thus each school seemed to be backed by science. The emotional-speech theory has been held in a vague way, indeed, by most of those theorists whose natural conservatism would have drawn them in the other direction, and is doubtless responsible for the attempts at mediation, first made by Ambros,[1] and now met in almost all musical literature. Music may be, and is, expressive, it is said, so long as each detail allows itself to be entirely derived from and justified by the mere formal element. The "centre of gravity" lies in the formal relations.

To this, after all, Hanslick himself might subscribe. Other writers seek to balance form and expression, insisting on "the dual nature of music," while resting ultimately on the emotional-speech theory. "The most universal composers, recognizing the interdependence of the two elements, produce the highest type of pure music, music in which beauty is based upon expression, and expression transfigured by beauty."[2]

This usual type of reconciliation, however, is a perfectly mechanical binding together of two possibly conflicting æsthetic demands. The question is of the essential nature of music, not whether music may be, but whether it must be, expressive;

[1] *The Boundaries of Music and Poetry.*
[2] D. G. Mason, *From Grieg to Brahms*, 1902, p. 30.

not whether it has expressive power, but whether it is, in its essence, expression, — a question which is only obscured by insisting on the interdependence of the two elements. If music has its essential source in the cadences of speech, if its aim is to be a glorified speech, then it must develop and must be judged accordingly. Herbert Spencer is perfectly logical in saying "It may be shown that music is but an idealization of the natural language of emotion, and that, consequently, music must be good or bad according as it conforms to the laws of this natural language." [1] But what, then, of music which, according to Ambros, is justified by its formal relations? Is music good because it is very expressive, and bad because it is too little expressive? or is its goodness and badness independent of its expressiveness? Such a question is not to be answered by recognizing two kinds of goodness. Only by an attempt to decide the fundamental nature of the musical experience, and an adjustment of the other factors in strict subordination to it, can the general principle be settled.

The excuse for this artificial yoking together of two opposing principles is apparent when it is seen that form and expression are taken as addressing themselves to two different mental faculties. It seems to be the view of most musical theorists that the experience of musical form is a perception, while the experience of musical expression, disre-

[1] *On Education*, p. 41.

garding for the moment the suggestion of facts and ideas, is an emotion. Thus Mr. Mason: " In music we are capable of learning, and knowledge of the principles of musical effect can help us to learn, that the balance and proportion and symmetry of the whole is far more essential than any poignancy, however great, in the parts. He best appreciates music . . . who understands it intellectually as well as feels it emotionally ; " [1] and again, " We feel in the music of Haydn its lack of emotional depth, and its lack of intellectual subtlety."

It is just this contrast and parallelism of structure as balance, proportion, symmetry, addressed to the mind, with expression as emotional content, that a true view of the æsthetic experience would lead us to challenge. If there is one thing that our study of the general nature of æsthetic experience has shown, it is that æsthetic emotion is unique — neither a perception nor an intellectual grasp of relations, nor an emotion within the accepted rubric — joy, desire, triumph, etc. Whether or not music is an exception to this principle, remains to be seen ; but the presumption is at least in favor of a direct, immediate, unique emotion aroused by the true beauty of music, whatever that may prove to be.

With a great literature in the form of special studies, we must yet, on the whole, admit that we possess no general formula in the philosophy or

[1] *Op. cit.*, p. 6.

psychology of music which covers the whole ground. Schopenhauer has said that music is the objectification of the will — not a copy or a picture of it, but the will itself; a doctrine which however illuminating when it is modified in various ways is obviously no explanation of our experience. Hanslick has but shown what music is not; Edmund Gurney's eloquent book, "The Power of Sound," is completely agnostic in its conclusion that music is a unique, indefinable, indescribable phenomenon, which possesses, indeed, certain analogues with other physical and psychical facts, but is coextensive with none. Spencer's theory of music as glorified speech is not only in as yet unexplained conflict with many facts, but has never been formulated so that it could apply to concrete cases. The same is true of Wagner's "music as the utterance of feeling."

But there is a body of scientific facts respecting the elements of music, in which we may well seek for clues. As facts alone they are of no value. They must be explained as completely as possible; and it is probable that if we are able to reach the ultimate nature and origin of these elements of music they will prove significant, and a way will be opened to a theory of the whole musical experience. The need of such intensive understanding must excuse the more or less technical discussions in the following pages, without which no firm foundation for a theory of music could be attained.

II

The two great factors of music are rhythm and tone-sensation, of which rhythm appears to be the more fundamental.

Rhythm is defined in general as a repeating series of time intervals. Events which occur in such a series are said to have rhythm. In æsthetics, it is the periodic recurrence of stress, emphasis, or accent in the movements of dancing, the sounds of music, the language of poetry. Subjectively it is the quality of stimulation due to a succession of impressions (tactual and auditory are most favorable) which vary regularly in objective intensity. We desire to understand the nature, and the source of the pleasing quality, of this phenomenon.

It is only by a complete psychological description, however, even a physiological explanation, that we can hope to fathom the tremendous significance of rhythm in music and poetry. Those treatments which expose its development in the dance and song really beg the question ; they assume the very fact for which we have to find the ground, namely, the natural impulse to rhythm. Even those theories which explain it as a helpful social phenomenon, as regulating work, etc., fail to account for its peculiar psychological character — that compelling, intimate force, the "Zwang" of which Nietszche speaks, which we all feel, and which makes it helpful. This compelling quality of rhythm would lead us to look behind the sociological influences, for the explanation in some fundamental condition of consciousness, some " demand " of the organism. For this reason we must find superficial the views which connect rhythm with the symmetry of the body as making rhythmical gesture necessary; or more particularly with the conditions of work, which, if it is skilled and well carried out, proceeds in equal recurring periods, like the swinging of a hammer or an axe. But it appears that primitive effort is not carried on in this way, and proceeds, not from regularity to rhythm, but rather, through, by means of rhythm, which is made a help, to regularity. Again, it is said that work can be well carried out by a large number of people, only in unison, only by simultaneous action, and that rhythm is a condition of this. The work in the cotton fields, the work of sailors, etc., requires something to give notice of the moment for beginning action. Rhythm would then have arisen as a social function. Against this it may be said that signals of this kind might assist common action without recurring at regular intervals, while periodicity is the fundamental quality of rhythm. Thus this theory would explain a natural tendency by its effect.

Looking then, in accordance with the principle stated above, for deeper conditions, we find rhythm explained in connection with such rhythmical events as the heart beat and pulse, the double rhythm of the breath; but these are, for the most part, unfelt; and moreover, they would hardly explain the predominance of rhythms quite other than the physiological ones. Another theory, closely allied, connects rhythm with the conditions of activity in general, but attaches itself rather to the effect of rhythm than to its cause. Thus we are reminded of the "heightened sense of expansion, or life, connected with the augmentation of muscular movements induced by the more extensive nervous discharges following rhythmic stimulation." [1] But why should it be just rhythmic stimulation that produces this effect? We are finally thrown back on physiology for the answer that in rhythmical stimulation there are involved recurrent activities of organs refreshed by immediately preceding periods of repose. Here again, however, we must ask, why on this hypothesis the periods themselves must be exactly equal. For within the periods the greatest variety obtains. One measure of a single note may be succeeded by another containing eight; within the periods, that is, the minor moments of activity and repose are quite unequal.

Last of all, we must note the view of rhythm as a phenomenon of expectation (Wundt). But while we can undoubtedly describe rhythm in terms of expectation and its satisfaction, rhythm is rhythm just through its difference from other kinds of expectation.

[1] H. R. Marshall, *Pain, Pleasure, and Æsthetics.*

All these explanations seem either merely to describe the facts we seek to explain, or to fail to notice the peculiar intimate nature of the rhythmical experience. But if it could be shown not only that in all stimulation there must be involved an alternation of activity and repose, but also that an equality of such periods was highly favorable to the organism, we should have the conditions for a physiological theory of rhythm. Now the important psychological facts of so-called subjective rhythmizing seem to supply just this need.

It has been shown [1] that we can neither receive objectively equal sense-stimuli, nor produce regular movements, without injecting into these a rhythmical element. A series of objectively equal sound-stimuli — the ticking of a clock, for instance — is heard in groups, within each of which one element is of greater intensity. A series of movements are never objectively equal, but grouped in the same way. Now this subjective rhythm, sensory and motor, is explained as follows from the general physiological basis of attention.

Attention itself is ultimately a motor phenomenon. Thus: the sensory aspect of attention is vividness, and vividness is explained physiologically as a brain-state of readiness for motor discharge ; [2] in

[1] T. L. Bolton, *Amer. Jour. of Psychol.*, vol. vi. The classical historical study of theories of rhythm remains that of Meumann, *Phil. Studien*, vol. x.

[2] Münsterberg, *Grundzüge d. Psychologie*, 1902, p. 525.

the case of a visual stimulus, for instance, a state of readiness to carry out movements of adjustment to the object; in short, the motor path is open. Now attention, or vividness, is found to fluctuate periodically, so that in a series of objectively equal stimuli, certain ones, regularly recurring, would be more vividly sensed. This is exemplified in the well-known facts of the fluctuation of the threshold of sensation, of the so-called retinal rivalry, and of the subjective rhythmizing of auditory stimuli, already mentioned. There is a natural rhythm of vividness. Here, therefore, in the very conditions of consciousness itself, we have the conditions of rhythm too. The case of subjective motor rhythm would be still clearer, since vividness is only the psychical side of readiness for motor discharge; in other words, increased readiness for motor discharge occurs periodically, giving motor rhythm.

It has been said [1] that this periodicity of the brain-wave cannot furnish the necessary condition for rhythm, inasmuch as it is itself a constant, and could at most be applied to a series which was adapted to its own time. But this objection does not fit the facts. The "brain-wave," or "vividness," or attention period, is not a constant, but attaches itself to the contents of consciousness. In other words, it does not function without material. It is itself conditioned by its occasion. In the case

[1] J. B. Miner, "Motor, Visual, and Applied Rhythms," *Psychol. Rev., Mon. Suppl.*, No. 21.

of a regularly repeated stimulus, it is simply adjusted to what is there, and out of the series
chooses, as it were, one at regular periods.[1]

Closely connected with these facts, perhaps only
a somewhat different aspect of them, is the phenomenon of motor mechanization. Any movement
repeated tends to become a circular reaction, as it
is called ; that is, the end of one repetition serves
as a cue for the beginning of the next. Now, in
regularly recurring stimuli, giving rise, as will be
later shown, to motor reactions, which are differentiated through the natural periodicity of the
attention (physiologically the tendency to motor
discharge), we have the best condition for this
mechanization. In other words, a rhythmical grouping once set up naturally tends to persist. The
organism prepares itself for shocks at definite
times, and shocks coming at those times are pleasant because they fulfill a need. Moreover, every
further stimulus reinforces the original activity ;
so that rhythmical grouping tends not only to persist, but to grow more distinct, — as, indeed, all
the facts of introspection show.

All this, however, is true of the repetition of
objectively equal stimuli. It shows how an impulse
to rhythm would arise and persist subjectively, but

---

[1] Facts, too technical for reproduction here, quoted by R. H.
Stetson (*Harvard Psychol. Studies*, vol. i., 1902) from Cleghorn's
and Hofbauer's experiments seem to be in harmony with this
view.

does not of itself explain the pleasure in the experience of objective rhythm. It may be said in general, however, that changes which would occur naturally in an objectively undifferentiated content give direct pleasure when they are artificially introduced, — when, that is, the natural disposition is satisfied. This we have seen to be true in the case of color contrast; and it is perhaps even more valid in the realm of motor activity. Whatever in sense stimulation gives the condition for, helps, furthers, enhances the natural function, is felt both as pleasing and as furthering the particular activity in question. Now, the objective stress in rhythm is but emphasis on a stress that would be in any case to some degree subjectively supplied. Rhythm in music, abstracting from all other pleasure-giving factors, is then pleasurable because it is in every sense a favorable stimulation.

In accordance with the principle that complete explanation of psychical facts is possible only through the physiological substrate, we have so far kept rather to that field in dealing with the foundations of our pleasure in rhythm. But further description of the rhythmical experience is most natural in psychological terms. There seems, indeed, on principle no ground for the current antithesis, so much emphasized of late, of " psychical " and "motor" theories of rhythm. Attention and expectation are not " psychical " as opposed to " motor." Granting, as no doubt most psychologists

would grant, that attention is the psychical analogue
of the physiological tendency to motor discharge,
then a motor automatism of which one is fully
conscious could be described as expectation and its
satisfaction. Indeed, the impossibility of a sharp
distinction between ideas of movement and movement sensations confirms this view. When expectation has reference to an experience with a movement element in it, the expectation itself contains
movement sensations of the kind in question.[1]
To say, then, that rhythm is expectation based on
the natural functioning of the attention period, is
simply to clothe our physiological explanation in
terms of psychological description. The usual
motor theory is merely one which neglects the
primary disposition to rhythm through attention
variations, in favor of the sensations of muscular
tension (kinæsthetic sensations) which arise *in*
rhythm, but do not cause it. To say that the impression of rhythm arises only in kinæsthetic sensations begs the question in the way previously
noted. Undoubtedly, the period once established,
the rhythmic group is held together, felt as a unit,
by means of the coördinated movement sensations ;
but the main problem, the possibility of this first
establishment, is not solved by such a motor theory.
In other words, the attention theory is the real
motor theory.

[1] C. M. Hitchcock, " The Psychol. of Expectation," *Psychol.
Rev., Mon. Suppl.*, No. 20.

Expectation is the " set " of the attention. Automatism is the set of the motor centres. Now as attention is parallel to the condition of the motor centres, we are able to equate expectation and automatic movement. Rhythm is literally embodied expectation, fulfilled. It is therefore easily to be understood that whatever other emotions connect themselves with satisfied expectation are at their ideal poignance in the case of rhythm.

It is from this point of view that we must understand the helpfulness of rhythm in work. That all definite stimulus, and especially sound stimulus, rhythmical or not, sets up a diffusive wave of energy, increasing blood circulation, dynamogenic phenomena, etc., is another matter, which has later to be discussed. But the essential is that this additional stimulus is rhythmical, and therefore a reinforcement of the nervous activity, and therefore a lightening and favorable condition of work itself. So it is, too, that we can understand the tremendous influence of rhythm just among primitive peoples, and those of a low degree of culture. Work is hard for savages, not because bodily effort is hard, but because the necessary concentration of attention is for them almost impossible; and the more, that in work they are unskilled, and without good tools, so that generally every movement has to be especially attended to. Now rhythm in work is especially directed to lighten that effort which they feel as hardest; it rests, renews, and frees the attention. Rhythm is helpful not primarily because it enables many to work together by making effort simultaneous, but rhythm rests and encourages the individual, and working together is most naturally carried out in rhythm.

To this explanation all the other factors of life-enhancement, etc., can be attached. Rhythm is undoubtedly favorable stimulation. Can it be brought under the full æsthetic formula of favorable stimulation with repose? A rhythm once established has both retrospective and prospective reference. It looks before and after, it binds together the first and the last moments of activity, and can therefore truly be said to return upon itself, so as to give a sense of equilibrium and repose.

But when we turn from the fundamental facts of simple rhythm to the phenomena of art we find straightway many other problems. It is safe to say that no single phrase of music or line of poetry is without variation; more, that a rhythm without variation would be highly disagreeable. How must we understand these facts? It is impossible within the natural limitations of this chapter to do more than glance at a few of them.

First of all, then, the most striking thing about the rhythmical experience is that the period, or group, is felt as a unit. " Of the number and relation of individual beats constituting a rhythmical sequence there is no awareness whatever on the part of the æsthetic subject. . . . Even the quality of

the organic units may lapse from distinct consciousness, and only a feeling of the form of the whole
sequence remains." [1] Yet the slightest deviation
from its form is remarked. Secondly, every variation creates not only a change in its own unit, but
a wave of disturbance all along the line. Also,
every variation from the type indicates a point of
accentual stress; the syncopated measure, for instance, is always strongly accented. All these facts
would seem to be connected with the view of the
importance of movement sensations in building up
the group feeling. The end of each rhythm period
gives the cue for the beginning of the next, and
the muscle tensions are coördinated within each
group; so that each group is really continuous,
and would naturally be "felt" as one, — but being automatic, would not be perceived in its separate elements. On the other hand, it is just automatic reaction, a deviation from which is felt most
strongly. The syncopated measure has to maintain itself against pressure, as it were, and thus
by making its presence in consciousness felt more
strongly, it emphasizes the fundamental rhythm
form.

This is well shown in the following passage from
a technical treatise on expression in the playing of
music. "The efforts which feeling makes to hold
to . . . the shape of the first rhythm, the force

[1] R. MacDougall, "The Structure of Simple Rhythm Forms,"
Harv. Psychol. Studies, vol. i., p. 332.

which it is necessary to use to make it lose its desires and its habits, and to impose others on it, are naturally expressed by an agitation, that is, by a crescendo or greater intensity of sound, by an acceleration in movement." [1] If a purely technical expression may be pardoned here, it could be said that the motor image,[2] that is, the coördinated muscular tensions which make the group feeling of the fundamental rhythm, is always latent, and becomes conscious whenever anything conflicts with it. Thus it is that we can understand the tremendous rhythmical consciousness in that music which seems most to contradict the fundamental rhythm, as in negro melodies, and rag-time generally; and in general, the livening effect of variation. The motor tension, the " set " becomes felt the moment there is objective interference — just as we feel the rhythm of our going downstairs only when we fail to get the sensation we expect.

This principle of the motor image is of tremendous significance, as we shall see, for the whole theory of music. Let it be sufficient to note here that expectation, in the form of *Gestaltsqualität*, or motor image, is, as a principle, sufficient for the explanation of the most important factors in the experience of rhythm.

[1] M. Lussy, *Traité de l' Expression Musicale*, Paris, 1874, p. 7.
[2] *Gestaltsqualität*, literally form-quality.

III

But we have dwelt too long on the general characteristics. Although our examples have been drawn mostly from the field of music, the preceding principles apply to all kinds of rhythm, tactual and visual as well as auditory. It is time to show why the rhythm out of all comparison the strongest, most compelling, most full of emotional quality, is the rhythm of music.

It has long been known that there is especially close connection between sounds and motor innervations. All sorts of sensorial stimuli produce reflex contractions, but the auditory, apparently, to a much higher degree. Animals are excited to all sorts of outbreaks by noise; children are less alarmed by visual than by auditory impressions. The fact that we dance to sound rather than to the waving of a baton, or rhythmical flashes of light for instance — the fact that this second proposition is felt at once to be absurd, shows how intimately the two are bound together. The irresistible effects of dance, martial music, etc., are trite commonplaces; and I shall therefore not heap up instances which can be supplied by every reader from his own experience. Now all this is not hard to understand, biologically. The eye mediated the information of what was far enough away to be fled from, or prepared for; the ear what was likely to be nearer, unseen, and so more ominous. As more ominous, it would have to be responded to in action more quickly. So that if any sense was to be in especially close connection with the motor centres, it would naturally be hearing.

The development of the auditory functions points to the same close connection of sound and movement. Sounds affect us as tone, and as impulse. The primitive sensation was one of impulse alone, mediated by the "shake-organs." These shake-organs at first only gave information about the attitude and movements of the body, and were connected with motor centres so as to be able to reëstablish equilibrium by means of reflexes. The original "shake-organ" developed into the organs of hearing and of equilibrium (that is, the cochlea and the semicircular canals respectively), but these were still side by side in the inner ear, and the close connection with the motor centres was not lost. Anatomically, the auditory nerve not only goes to those parts of the brain whence the motor innervation emanates, and to the reflex centres in the cerebellum, but passes close by the vagus or pneumogastric nerve, which rules the heart and the vasomotor functions. We have then multiplied reasons for the singular effect of sound on motor reactions, and on the other organic functions which have so much to do with feeling and emotion.

Every sound-stimulus is then much more than sound-sensation. It causes reflex contractions in the whole muscular system; it sets up some sort of cardiac and vascular excitation. This reaction is in general in the direction of increased amplitude of respiration, but diminution of the pulse, depending on a peripheral vaso-constriction. Moreover, this vasomotor reaction is given in a melody or piece of music, not by its continuity, but for every one of the variations of rhythm, key, or intensity, — which is of interest in the light of what has been said of the latent motor image. The obstacle in syncopated rhythm is physiologically translated as vaso-constriction. In general, music induces cardiac acceleration.

All this is of value in showing how completely the attention-motor theory of rhythm applies to the rhythm of sounds. Since sound is much more than sound, but sound-sensation, movement, and visceral change together, we can see that the rhythmical experience of music is, even more literally and completely than at first appeared, an *embodied* expectation. No sensorial rhythm could be so completely induced in the psychophysical organism as the sound-rhythm. In listening to music, we see how it is that we ourselves, body and soul, seem to be *in* the rhythm. We make it, and we wait to make it. The satisfaction of our expectation is like the satisfaction of a bodily desire or need; no, not like it, it *is* that. The conditions and causes of rhythm and our pleasure in it are more deeply seated than language, custom, even instinct;

they are in the most fundamental functions of life. This element of music, at least, seems not to have arisen as a " natural language."

IV

The facts of the relations of tones, the elements, that is, of melody and harmony, are as follows. We cannot avoid the observation that certain tones " go together," as the phrase is, while others do not. This peculiar impression of belonging together is known as consonance, or harmony. The intervals of the octave, the fifth, the third, for instance, that is, C–C′, C–G, C–E, in the diatonic scale, are harmonious ; while the interval of the second, C–D, is said to be dissonant. Consonance, however, is not identical with pleasingness, for different combinations are sometimes pleasing, sometimes displeasing. In the history of music we know that the octave was to the Greeks the most pleasing combination, to mediæval musicians the fifth, while to us, the third, which was once a forbidden chord, is perhaps most delightful. Yet we should never doubt that the octave is the most consonant, the fifth and the third the lesser consonant of combinations. We see, thus, that consonance, whatever its nature, is independent of history ; and we must seek for its explanation in the nature of the auditory process.

Various theories have been proposed. That of

Helmholtz has held the field so long that, although weighty objections have been raised to it, it must still be treated with respect. In introducing it a short review of the familiar facts of the physics and physiology of hearing may not be out of place.

The vibration rates per second of the vibrating bodies, strings, steel rods, etc., which produce those musical tones which are consonant, are in definite and small mathematical ratios to each other. Thus the rates of C–C′ are as $1:2$; of C–G, C–E, as $2:3$, $4:5$. In general, the simpler the fraction, the greater the consonance.

But no sonorous body vibrates in one single rate; a taut string vibrates as a whole, which gives its fundamental tone, but also in halves, in fourths, etc., each giving out a weaker partial tone, in harmony with the fundamental. And according to the different ways in which a sonorous body divides, that is, according to the different combination of partial tones peculiar to it, is its especial quality of tone, or timbre. The whole complex of fundamental and partial tones is what we popularly speak of as a tone, — more technically a clang. These physical agitations or vibrations are transmitted to the air. Omitting the account of the anatomical path by which they reach the inner ear, we find them at last setting up vibrations in a many-fibred membrane, the basilar membrane, which is in direct connection with the ends of the auditory nerve. It is supposed that to every possible rate of vibration, that is, every possible tone, or partial tone, there corresponds a fibre of the basilar membrane fitted by its length to vibrate synchronously with the original wave-elements. The complex wave is thus analyzed into its constituents. Now when two tones, which we will for clearness suppose to be simple, unaccompanied by partial tones, sounding together, have vibration rates in simple ratios to each other, the air-waves set in motion do not interfere with each other, but combine into a complex but homogeneous wave. If they have to each other a complicated ratio, such as 500 : 504, the air-waves will not only not coalesce, but four times in the second the trough of one wave will meet the crest of the other, thus making the algebraic sum zero, and producing the sensation of a momentary stoppage of the sound. When these stoppages, or beats, as they are called, are too numerous to be heard separately, as in the interval, say, 500 : 547, the effect is of a disagreeable roughness of tone, and this we call discord. In other words, any tones which do not produce beats are harmonious, or harmony is the absence of discord. In the words of Helmholtz,[1] consonance is a continuous, dissonance an intermittent, tone-sensation.

Aside from the fact that consonance, as a psychological fact, seems positive, while this determination is negative, two very important facts can be

---

[1] *Lehre v. d. Tonempfindungen,* p. 370, in 4th edition.

set up in opposition. As a result of experimental investigation, we know that the impression of consonance can accompany the intermittent or rough sound-sensations we know as beating tones; and, conversely, tones can be dissonant when the possibility of beats is removed. Briefly, it is possible to make beats without dissonance, and dissonance without beats.

The other explanation makes consonance due to the identity of partial tones. When two tones have one or more partial tones in common they are said to be related; the amount of identity gives the degree of relationship. Physiologically, one or more basilar membrane fibres are excited by both, and this fact gives the positive feeling of relationship or consonance. Of course the obvious objection to this view is that the two tones should be felt as differently consonant when struck on instruments which give different partial tones, such as organ and piano, while in fact they are not so felt.

But it is not after all essential to the æsthetics of music that the physiological basis of harmony should be fully understood. The point is that certain tones do indeed seem to be "preordained to congruity," preordained either in their physical constitution or their physiological relations, and not to have achieved congruity by use or custom. Consonance is an immediate and fundamental impression, — psychologically an ultimate fact. That it

is ultimate is emphasized by Stumpf [1] in his theory
of Fusion. Consonance is fusion, that is, unitary
impression. Fusion is not identical with inability
to distinguish two tones from each other in a chord,
although this may be used as a measure of fusion.
Consonance is the feeling of unity, and fusion is
the mutual relation of tones which gives that feeling.

The striking fact of modern music is the principle of tonality. Tonality is said to be present in a
piece of music when every element in it is referred
to, gets its significance from its relation to, a fundamental tone, the tonic. The tonic is the beginning
and lowest note in the scale in question, and all
notes and chords are understood according to their
place in that scale. But the conception of the scale
of course does not cover the ground, it merely furnishes the point of departure, — the essential is
in the reference of every element to the fundamental tone. The tonic is the centre of gravity of a
melody.

The feeling of tonality grew up as follows.
Every tone was referred to a fundamental, whether
or not it made with it an harmonious interval. The
fundamental was imaged *together with* every other
note, and when a group of such references often
appeared together, the feelings bound up with the
single reference (interval-feelings) fused into a

[1] *Beiträge zur Akustik u. Musikwissenschaft*, Heft I, Konso-
nanz u. Dissonanz, 1898.

single feeling, — the tonality-feeling. When this point is once reached, it is clear that every tone is heard not as itself alone, but in its relations; it is not that we judge of tonality, it is a direct impression, based on a psychological principle that we have already touched on in the theory of rhythm. The tonality-feeling is a feeling of form, or motor image, just as the shape of objects is a motor image. We do not now need to go through all possible experiences in relation to these objects; we *possess* their form in a system of motor images, which are themselves only motor cues for coördinated movements. So every tone is felt as something at a certain distance from, with a certain relation to, another tone which is dimly imagined. In following a melody, the notes are able to belong together for us by virtue of the background of the tone to which they are related, and in terms of which they are heard. The tonality is indeed literally a " funded content," — that is, a funded capital of relations.

These are the general facts of tonality. But what is its meaning for the nature of music? Why should all notes be referred to one? Is this, too, an ultimate psychological fact? In answer there may be pointed out the original basic quality of certain tones, and the desire we have to return to them. Of two successive tones, it is always the one which is, in the ratio of their vibration rates, a power of two, with which we wish to end.[1] When

[1] Max Meyer, *A Psychological Theory of Melody.*

neither of two successive tones contains a power of two, we have no preference as to the ending. Thus denoting any tone by 1, it is always to 1 or 2, or 2^n that we wish to return, from any other possible tone ; while 3 and 5, 5 and 7, leave us indifferent as to their succession. In general, when two tones are related, as $2^n : 3, 5, 7, 9, 15$ — in which 2^n denotes every power of two, including $2^o = 1$, with the progression from the first to the second, there is bound up a tendency to return to the first. Thus the fundamental fact of melodic sequence may be said to be the primacy of 2 in vibration rates. But 2^n, in a scale containing 3, 5, etc., is always what we know as the tonic. The tonic, then, gives a sense of equilibrium, of rest, of finality, while to end on another tone gives a feeling of restlessness or striving.

Now tone-relationship alone, it is clear, would not of itself involve this immediate impulse to end a sequence of notes on one rather than on another. Nor is tonality, in the all-pervasive sense in which we understand it, a characteristic of ancient, or of mediæval music, while the tendency to end on a certain tone, which we should to-day call the tonic, was always felt. Thus, since complete tonality was developed late in the history of music, while the closing on the tonic was certainly prior to it, the finality of the tonic would seem to be the primary fact, out of which the other has been developed.

We speak to-day, for instance, of dissonant

chords, which call for a resolution — and are inclined to interpret them as dissonant just because
they do so call. But the desire for resolution is
historically much later than the distinction between
consonance and dissonance. . . . " What we call
resolution is not change from dissonant to consonant *in general*, but the transition of definite tones
of a dissonant interval into *definite tones* of a
consonant." [1] The dissonance comes from the device of getting variety, in polyphonic music, by
letting some parts lag behind, and the discords
which arose while they were catching up were resolved in the final coming together; but the *steps*
were all *predetermined*. [2] Resolution was inevitably
implied by the very principle on which the device
is founded. That is, the understanding of a chord
as something *to be resolved*, is indeed part of the
feeling of tonality; but the ending on the tonic
was that out of which this resolution-feeling grew.

Must we, then, say that the finality of the tonic
is a unique, inexplicable phenomenon? giving up
the nature of melody as a problem if not insoluble,
at least unsolved?

The feeling of finality in the return to 2^n is explained by Lipps and his followers, from the fact
that the two-division is most natural, and so tones
of 2^n vibrations would have the character of rest
and equilibrium. This explanation might hold if

[1] Stumpf, *op. cit.*, p. 33.
[2] Grove, *Dict. of Music and Musicians*. Art. "Resolution."

we were ever conscious of the two-division as such, in tones — which we are not; so that it would seem to depend on the restful character of a perception which by hypothesis is never present to the mind at all.

The experience is, on the contrary, immediate, — an impression, not a perception; and this immediacy points to the one ultimate fact in musical feeling we have so far discovered. The whole development of the scale, and the complex feeling of tonality, is an expression of the desire for consonance. Every change and correction in the scale has gone to make every note more consonant with its neighbors. And naturally the tonic is the tone with which all other tones have the most unity. Now this " return " phenomenon is a simpler case of the desire for the feeling of unity. The tonic is the epitome of all the most perfect feelings of consonance or unity which are possible in any particular sequence of tones, and is therefore the goal or resting-place after an excursion. The undoubted feeling of equilibrium or repose which we have in ending on the tonic is thus explained. Not that consonance itself, the feeling of unity, is explained. But at any rate consonance is the root of the " return," and of its development into complete tonality.

The history of music is then the explicit development of acoustic laws implicit in every stage of musical feeling. That feeling covers an ever wider field. When Mr. Hadow says that the terms concord and discord are wholly relative to the ear of the listener,[1] and that the distinction between them is not to be explained on any mathematical basis, or by any *a priori* law of acoustics, — that it is not because a minor second is ugly that we dislike it, for it will be a concord some day, — he is only partly right. The minor second may be a "concord," that is, we may like it, some day; but that will be because we have extended our feeling of tonality to include the minor second. When that day comes the minor second will be so closely linked with other fully consonant combinations that we shall hear it in terms of them, just as to-day we hear the chord of the dominant seventh in terms of its resolution. But the basis will not be convention or custom, except in so far as custom is the unfolding of natural law. The course of music, like that of every other art, is away from arbitrary — though simple — convention, to a complexity which satisfies the natural demands of the organism. The "natural persuasion" of the ear is omnipotent.

V

It has been said above that the feeling of tonality is a motor image or "form-quality" and that the image of the tonic persists throughout every sequence of tones in a melody. Now these are not only felt as having a certain relation to the tonic;

[1] W. H. Hadow, *Studies in Modern Music*, 1893.

that relation is an active one. It was said that we had a positive desire to end on a certain tone, and that a tendency to pass to that tone was bound up with the hearing of another tone. The degree of this tendency is determined by their relation. The key, the tonality, is determined by the consensus of intervals which have been felt as more or less consonant. Then steps in this scale which come near to the great salient points — that is, the points of greatest consonance, which is unity, which is rest — are felt as suggesting them. This is the reason why a semitone progression is felt as so compelling. In taking the scale upward, C to C', that element in the tone-space already clearly foreshadowed by the previous tones is C'; B is so near that it is almost C' — it seems to cry aloud to be completed by C'. Then the tendency to move from B to C' is especially strong. In the same way a chromatic note suggests most strongly the salient point in the scheme to which it is nearest — and " tends " to it as to a point of comparative rest. The difference between the major and minor scales may be found in the lesser definiteness [1] with which the tendency to progression, in the latter, is felt — " a condition of hovering, a kind of ambiguity, of doubt, to which side the movement shall proceed." We may then understand a melody as ever tending with various degrees of urgency, of strain, to its centre of gravity, the tonic.

[1] F. Weinmann, *Zeitschr. f. Psychol.*, Bd. 35, p. 360.

It is from this point of view that we can see the
cogency of Gurney's remark, that when music
seems to be yearning for unutterable things, it is
really yearning only for the next note. " In this
step from the state of rest into movement and return, the coming again to rest; on what circuitous
ways, with what reluctances and hesitations; whether
quick and decisively or gradually and unnoticed —
therein consists the nature of melody." [1]

Or in Gurney's more eloquent description, " The
melody may begin by pressing its way through a
sweetly yielding resistance to a gradually foreseen
climax; whence again fresh expectation is bred,
perhaps for another excursion, as it were, round
the same centre but with a bolder and freer sweep,
. . . to a point where again the motive is suspended
on another temporary goal; till after a certain
number of such involutions and evolutions, and of
delicately poised leanings and reluctances and yield-
ings, the forces so accurately measured just suffice
to bring it home, and the sense of potential and
coming integration which has underlain all our
provisional adjustments of expectation is trium-
phantly justified." [2]

This should not be taken as a more or less poet-
ical account under the metaphor of motion.   These
" leanings " are literal in the sense that one note
does imply another as its natural complement and
satisfaction and we seek to reach or make it.   The

[1] Weinmann, *op. cit.*   [2] *Op. cit.*, p. 165.

striving is an intrinsic element, not a by-product for our understanding.

There is another point to note. The " sense of potential and coming integration" is a strong factor of melody. If it cannot be said that the first note implies the last, it is at least true that from point to point the next step is dimly foreseen, and this effect is cumulative. If melody is an ever-hindered striving for the goal, at least the hindrances themselves are stations on the way, each one as overcome adding to the final momentum with which the goal is reached. It is like an accumulation of evidence, a constellation of associations. AB foretells C; but ABCDEF rushes yet more strongly upon G. So it is that the irresistibleness, the " unalterable rightness" of a piece of music increases from beginning to end.

The significance of this essential internal necessity of progression cannot be overestimated. The unalterable rightness of music is founded on natural acoustic laws, and this "rightness" is fundamental. A melody is not right because it is beautiful, it is beautiful because it is right. The natural tendencies point out different paths to the goal; therefore there are different ways of being right, and thus different ways of being beautiful; but the nature of the relation between point and point, the nature of the progression, that is, the nature of melody, is the same.

Up to this point we have consistently abstracted

from the element of rhythm in melody. Strictly speaking, however, it is impossible to do so. The individuality of a melody is absolutely dependent on its rhythm, that is, on the relative time-value of its tones. Gurney has devoted some amusing pages to showing the trivial, dragging, lustreless tunes that result from ever so slight a change in the rhythm of noble themes, or even in the distribution of rhythmical elements within the bar. The reason for this is evident. The nature of melody in the sense of sequence consists in the varied answers to the demands of the ear as felt at each successive point. Now it is clear that such "answer" can be emphasized, given indifferently, held in suspense, in short, subjected to all kinds of variation as well by the rhythmical form into which it is cast, as by the different choice of possibilities for the tone itself. The rhythm helps out the melody not only by adding to it an independently pleasing element, but, and this is indeed the essential, by reinforcing the intrinsic relations of the notes themselves. Thus it is in the highest degree true that in melody and rhythm we do not have content and form, but that, strictly speaking, the melody is tone-sequence in rhythm.

The intimate bondage of tone-sequence and rhythm is grounded in the identity of their inner nature ; both are varieties of the objective conditions of embodied expectation. It is not of the essence of music to satisfy explicit and conscious expectation — to satisfy the understanding. It meets on the contrary a subconscious, automatic need which becomes conscious only in the moment of its contenting. Every moment of progress in a beautiful melody is hailed like an instinctive action performed for the first time. Rhythm is the ideal satisfaction of attention in general with all its bodily concomitants and expressions. Tone-sequence is the satisfaction of attention directed to auditory demands. But the form-quality of rhythm, the form-quality of tonality, is an all but subconscious possession. Together, reinforcing each other in melody, they furnish the ideal arrangement of the most poignant of sense-stimulations.

VI

It is strange that those who would accept the general facts of musical logic as outlined above do not perceive that they have thereby cut away the ground from under the feet of the "natural language" argument. If the principle of choice in the progress of a melody is tone-relationship, the principle of choice cannot also be the cadences of the speaking voice. That musical intervals often *recall* the speaking voice is another matter, as we have said, and to this it may be added that they much more often do not. The question here is only of the primacy of the principle. Thus it would seem that the facts of musical structure constitute in themselves a refutation of the view we have disputed.

To say that music arose in " heightened speech "
is irrelevant ; for the occasion of an æsthetic
phenomenon is never its cause. It might as well
be said that music arose in economic conditions,
— as indeed Grosse, in his " Anfänge der Kunst,"
conclusively shows, without attempting to make this
social occasion intrude into the nature of the phenomenon. Primitive decorative art arose in the
imitation of the totemic or clan symbols, mostly
animal forms ; but we have seen that the æsthetic
quality of the decoration is due to the demands of
the eye, and appears fully only in the comparative
degradation of the representative form. In exactly
the same way might we consider the " degradation "
of speech cadences into real music, — supposing this
were really the origin of music. As a matter of
fact, however, the best authorities seem to be
agreed that the primitive " dance-song " was rather
a monotonous, meaningless chant, and that the original pitch-elements were mechanically supplied by
the first musical instruments ; these being at first
merely for noise, and becoming truly vibrating, sonorous bodies because they were more easily struck
if they were hard or taut. The musical tones which
these hard vibrating bodies gave out were the first
determinations of pitch, and of the elements of the
scale, which correspond to the natural partial vibrations of such bodies. " The human voice," Wal-
laschek [1] tells us, " equally admits of any pentatonic

[1] *Primitive Music*, 1893, p. 156.

or heptatonic intervals, and very likely we should never have got regular scales if we had depended upon the ear and voice only. The first unique cause to settle the type of a regular scale is the instrument." To this material we have to apply only that "natural persuasion of the ear" which we have already explained, to account for the full development of music.

The beauty of music, in so far as beauty is identical with pleasantness, consists in its satisfaction of the demands of the ear, and of the whole psychophysical organism as connected with the ear. It is now time to return to a thread dropped at the beginning. It was said that a common way of settling the musical experience was to make musical beauty the object of perception, and musical expression the object, or source, of emotion. This view seems to attach itself to all shades of theory. Hanslick always contrasts intellectual activity as attaching to the form, and emotion as attaching to the sensuous material (that is, the physical effects of motion, loud or soft sound, tempo, etc.). He speaks of the æsthetic criterion of *intelligent* gratification. "The truly musical listener" has "his attention absorbed by the particular form and character of the composition," "the unique position which the *intellectual element* in music occupies in relation to *forms* and *substance* (subject)." M. Dauriac in the same way separates the emotion of music [1] as a pro-

[1] "Le Plaisir et l'Emotion Musicale," *Rev. Philos.*, Tome 42, No. 7.

duct of nervous excitations, from the appreciation of it as beautiful. " It is probable that the pleasure caused by rhythm and color prevails with a pretty large number, with the greatest number, over the pleasure in the musical form, pleasure too exclusively *psychological* for one to be content with it alone. . . . The musical sense implies the intelligence. . . . The theory . . . applies to a great number of sonorous sensations, and not at all to any musical perceptions." Mr. W. H. Hadow [1] tells us that it is the duty of the musician not to flatter the sense with an empty compliment of sound, but to reach through sensation to the mental faculties within. And again we read " the art of the composer is in a sense the discovery and exposition of the *intelligible* relations in the multifarious material at his command." [2]

Now it is not hard to see how this antithesis has come about. But that the work of a master is always capable of logical analysis does not prove that our apprehension of it is a logical act. And the preceding discussion has wholly failed to make its point, if it is not now clear that the musical experience is an impression and not a judgment; that the feeling of tonality is not a judgment of tonality, and that though the æsthetic enjoyment of music extends only to those limits within which the feeling of tonality is active, that feeling is more likely than not to be quite unintelligible to the listener.

[1] *Op. cit.*, p. 47.   [2] Grove's *Dict.* Art. "Relationship."

Indeed, if it were not so, we should have to restrict, by hypothesis, the enjoyment of music to those able to give a technical report of what they hear, — which is notoriously at odds with the facts. That psychologist is quite right who holds [1] that psychology, in laying down a principle explaining the actual effect of a musical piece, is not justified in confining itself to skilled musicians and taking no notice of more than nine tenths of those who listen to the piece. But on the understanding that the tonality-feeling acts subconsciously, that our satisfaction with the progression of notes is unexplained to ourselves, though explicable by the laws of acoustics and association, we are enabled to bring within the circle of those who have the musical experience even those nine tenths whose intellects are not actively participant.

The fact is that musical form, in the sense of structure, balance, symmetry, and proportion in the arrangement of phrases, and in the contrasting of harmonies and keys, is different from the musical form which is felt intimately, intrinsically, as the desired, the demanded progress from one note to another. Structure is indeed perceived, understood, enjoyed as an orderly unified arrangement. Form is felt as an immediate joy. Structure it is which many critics have in mind when they speak of form, and it is the confusion between the two which makes such an antithesis of musical beauty and sensuous

[1] Lazarus, *Das Leben der Seele*, ii, p. 323.

material possible. The real musical beauty, it is clear, is in the melodic idea; in the sequence of tones which are indissolubly one, which are felt together, one of which cannot exist without the other. Musical beauty is in the intrinsic musical form. And yet here, too, we must admit, that, in the last analysis, structure and form need not be different. The perfect structure will be such a unity that it, too, will be *felt* as one — not only " the orderly distribution of harmonies and keys in such a manner that the mind can realize the concatenation as a complete and distinct work of art." The ideal musical consciousness would have an ideally great range ; it would not only realize the concatenation, but it would take it in as one takes in a single phrase, a simple tune, retaining it from first note to last. The ordinary musical consciousness has merely a much shorter breath. It can " feel " an air, a movement; it cannot " feel " a symphony, it can only perceive the relation of keys and harmonies therein. With repeated hearing, study, experience, this span of beauty may be indefinitely extended — in the individual, as in the race. But no one will deny that the direct experience of beauty, the single æsthetic thrill, is measured exactly by the length of this span. It is only genius — hearer or composer — who can operate " à longue haleine."

So it is that we must understand the development in musical form from the cut and dried sonata

form to the wayward yet infinitely greater beauty
of Beethoven; and thence to the " free forms " of
modern music. " Infinite melody " is a contradiction in terms, because when the first term cannot
be present in consciousness with the last there is
nothing to control and direct the progression ; and
our musical memory is limited. Yet we can conceive, theoretically, the possibility of an indefinite
widening of the memory.

It was on some such grounds as these that Poe
laid down his famous " Poetic Principle," — that a
long poem does not exist; that " a long poem "
is simply a flat contradiction in terms. He says,
indeed, that because " elevating excitement," the
end of a poem, is " through a psychical necessity "
transient, therefore no poem should be longer than
the natural term of such excitement. It is clearly
possible to substitute for " elevating excitement,"
immediate musical feeling of the individual. What
is the meaning of " feeling," " impression," here ? It
is the power of entering into a *Gestaltsqualität* —
a motor group, a scheme in which every element is
the mechanical cue to the following. Beauty ceases
for the hearer where this carrying power, the
" funded capital " of tone-linkings ceases. In just
the same way, if rhythm were a perception rather
than an impression, we ought to be able to apprehend a rhythm of which the unit periods were
hours. Yet we may so bridge over the moments of
beauty in experience that we are enabled, without

stretching the figure to a breaking-point, to speak
of a symphony or an opera as a single beautiful
work of art.

VII

But what of the difficulties which such a theory
must meet? The most obvious one is the short life
of musical works. If musical beauty is founded in
natural laws, why does music so quickly grow old?
The answer is that music is a phenomenon of expectation as founded on these natural laws. It is
the tendency of one note to progress to another
which is the basis of the vividness of our experience. We expect, indeed, what belongs objectively
to the development of a melody, but only that
particular variety of progression to which we have
become accustomed. So it is that music which
presents only the old, simple progressions gives the
greatest sense of ease, but the least sense of effort —
the ideal motion not being hindered on its way. Intensity, vividness, would be felt where the progression is less obvious, but felt as " fitting in " when it
is once made ; and where it is not obvious at all —
where the link is not felt, a sense of dissatisfac-
tion and restlessness arises. So it is with music
which we know by heart. It is not that we know
each note, and so expect it, but that it is felt as
necessarily issuing out of the preceding. A piece of
poor music, really heterogeneous and unconnected,
might be thoroughly familiar, and yet never, in

this sense, felt as *satisfying* expectation. In the same way, music in which the progressions were germane to the existing tonality-feeling, while still not absolutely obvious, would not be less quickening to the musical sense, even if learned by heart. It is clear that there is an external and an internal expectation — one, imposed by memory, for the particular piece; the other constituted partly by intrinsic internal relations, partly by the degree to which these internal relations have been exploited. That is, the possibility of musical expectation, and pleasure in its satisfaction, is conditioned by the possession of a tonality-feeling which covers the constituents of the piece of music, but which has not become absolutely mechanical in its action. Just as rhythm needs an obstacle to make the structure felt, so melody needs some variation from the obvious set of relations already won and possessed. If that possession is too complete, the melody becomes as stale and uninteresting as would a 3–4 rhythm without a change or a break.

The test of genius in music, of the width and depth of mastery, is to be able to become familiar without ceasing to be strange. On the other hand, if in music to be great is always to be misunderstood, it is no less true, here as elsewhere, that to be misunderstood is not always to be great. And music may be merely strange, and pass into oblivion, without ever having passed that stage of surprised and delighted acceptance which is the test of its truth to fundamental laws.

But how shall music advance? How shall it set out to win new relations? It is at least conceivable that it takes the method of another art which we have just studied. To get new beauties, it does not say, — Go to, I will add to the beauties I already have! It makes new occasions, and by way of these finds the impulse it seeks. Renoir paints the *baigneuse* of Montmartre, and finds "the odd, beautiful huddle of lines" in so doing; Rodin portrays ever new subtleties of situation and mood, and by way of these comes most naturally to "the unedited poses." So a musician, we may imagine, comes to new and strange utterances by way of a new and strange motion or cry that he imitates. Out of the various bents and impulses that these give him he chooses the ones that chance to be beautiful. And in time these new beauties have become worn away like the trite metaphors that are now no longer metaphors, but part of the "funded capital." That was a ridiculous device of Schumann's, who found a *motif* for one of his loveliest things by using the letters of his temporary fair one's name — A B E G G; but it may not be so utterly unlike the procedure by which music grows.

VIII

But what provision must be made for the emotions of music? It cannot be that the majority of musicians, who are strangely enough the very ones to insist that music is merely the language of emotion, are utterly and essentially wrong. Nor has it been attempted to prove them so. The beauty of music, we have sought to show, grows and flowers out of tone-relations alone, consists in tone-sequences alone. But it has not been said that music did not arouse emotion, nor that it might not on occasion even express it.

It is in fact now rather a commonplace in musical theory, to show the emotional means which music has at its command; and I shall therefore be very brief in my reference to them. They may be shortly classed as expressive by association and by direct induction. Expressive by association are passages of direct imitation : the tolling of bells, the clash of arms, the roar of wind, the hum of spinning wheels, even to the bleating of sheep and the whirr of windmills; the cadence of the voice in pleading, laughter, love; from such imitations we are *reminded* of a fact or an emotion. More intimate is the expression by induction; emotion is aroused by activities which themselves form part of the emotions in question. Thus the differences in tempo, reproduced in nervous response, call up the gayety, sadness, hesitation, firmness, haste, growing excitement, etc., of which whole experiences these movement types form a part.

These emotions, as has often been shown, are absolutely general and indefinite in their character, and are, on the whole, even in their intensity, no measure of the beauty of the music which arouses them. Indeed, we can get intense emotion from sound which is entirely unmusical. So, too, loudness, softness, crescendo, diminuendo, volume, piercingness, have their emotional accompaniments. It is to Hanslick that we owe the general summing up of these possibilities of expression as " the dynamic figures of occurrences." How this dynamic skeleton is filled out through association, or that special form of association which we know as direct induction, is not hard to understand on psychological grounds. It is not necessary to repeat here the reasons for the literally " moving " appeal of sound-stimulations, which have been already detailed under the subject of rhythm.

Yet there still remains a residue of emotion not entirely accounted for. It has been said that these, the emotions expressed, or aroused, are more or less independent of the intrinsic musical beauty. But it cannot be denied that there is an intense emotion which grows with the measure of the beauty of a piece of music, and which music lovers are yet loth to identify with the so-called general æsthetic emotion, or with the " satisfaction of expectation," different varieties of which, in fusion, we have tried

to show as the basis of the musical experience. The
æsthetic emotion from a picture is not like this, they
say, and a mere satisfaction of expectation is unut-
terably tame. This is unique, æsthetic, individual!

I believe that the clue to this objection is the
natural impulse of mankind to confuse the intensity
of an experience with a difference in kind. But first
of all, there must be added to our list of definite
emotions from music, those which attach themselves
to the internal relations of the notes. Gurney has
said that when we feel ourselves yearning for the
unutterable, we are really yearning for the next
note. That is the secret! Each one of those tendencies, demands, leanings, strivings, returns, as
between tone and tone in a melody, is necessarily
accompanied by the feeling-tone which belongs to
such an attitude. And it is to be noted that all the
more poignant emotions we get from music are always stated in terms of urgency, of strain, of effort.
That is because these emotions, and these alone, are
inescapable in music since they are founded on the
intrinsic relations of the notes themselves. It is
just for this reason, too, that music, just in proportion to its beauty, is felt, as some one says, like
vinegar on a wound, by those in grief or anxiety.

"I shall loathe sweet tunes, where a note grown strong
    Relents and recoils, and climbs and closes."

It is the yearning that is felt most strongly, the
more vividly are the real musical relations of the
notes brought out.

Music expresses and causes tension, strain, yearning, through its inner, its "absolute" nature. But it does more; it satisfies these yearnings. It not only creates an expectation to satisfy it, but the expectation itself is of a poignant, emotional, personal character. What is the emotion that is aroused by such a satisfaction?

The answer to this question takes us back again to that old picturesque theory of Schopenhauer — that music is the objectification of the will. Schopenhauer meant this in a metaphysical, and to us an inadmissible sense; but I believe that the psychological analysis of the musical experience which we have just completed shows that there is another sense in which it is absolutely true.

The best psychological theory of the experience of volition makes it the imaging of a movement or action, followed by feelings of strain, and then of the movement carried out. The anticipation is the essential. Without anticipation, as in the reflex, winking, the action appears involuntary. Without the feeling of effort or strain, as in simply raising the empty hand, the self-feeling is weaker. When all these three elements, *image*, *effort*, *success*, are present most vividly, the feeling is of triumphant volition. Now my thesis is — the thesis toward which every thought of the preceding has pointed — that the fundamental facts of the musical experience are supremely fitted to bring about the illusion and the exaltation of the triumphant will.

The image, dimly foreshadowed, is given in the half-consciousness of each note as it appears, and in that sense of coming integration already recognized. The proof is the shock and disappointment when the wrong note is sounded; if we had not some anticipation of the right, the wrong one would not shock. The strain we have in the effort of the organism to reach the note, the tendency to which is implicit in the preceding. The success is given in the coming of the note itself.

All this is no less true of rhythm — but there the expectation is more mechanical, less conscious, as has been fully shown. The more beautiful, that is, the more inevitably, irresistibly right the music, the more powerful the influence to this illusion of the triumphant will. The exaltation of musical emotion is thus the direct measure of the perfection of the relations — the beauty of the music. This, then, is the only intimate, immediate, intrinsic emotion of music — the illusion of the triumphant will!

One word more on the interpretation of music in general æsthetic terms. All that has been said goes to show that music possesses to the very highest degree the power of stimulation. Can we attribute to it repose in any other sense than that of satisfying a desire that it arouses? We can do so in pointing out that music ever returns upon itself — that its motion is cyclic. Music is the art of auditory implications; but more than this, its last note returns to its first. It is as truly a unity as if it were static. We may say that the beauty of a picture is only entered into when the eye has roved over the whole canvas, and holds all the elements indirectly while it is fixated upon one point. In exactly the same way music is not beauty unless it is *all* there; at every point a fusion of the heard tone with the once heard tones in the order of their hearing. The melody, as a set of implications, is as *essentially* timeless as the picture. By melody too, then, is given the perfect moment, the moment of unity and completeness, of stimulation and repose.

The æsthetic emotion for music is then the favorable stimulation of the sense of hearing and those other senses that are bound up with it, together with the repose of perfect unity. It has a richer color, a more intense exaltation in the illusion of the triumphant will, which is indeed the peculiar mark of the perfect moment for the self in action.

VI

THE BEAUTY OF LITERATURE

VI

THE BEAUTY OF LITERATURE

I

THAT in the practice and pleasure of art for art's sake there lurks an unworthy element, is a superstition that recurs in every generation of critics. A most accomplished and modern disciple of the gay science but yesterday made it a reproach to the greatest living English novelist, that he, too, was all for beauty, all for art, and had no great informing purpose. " Art for art's sake " is clearly, to this critic's mind, compatible with the lack of something all desirable for novels. Yet if there is indeed a characteristic excellence of the novel, if there is something the lack of which in a novel is rightly deplored, then the real art for art's sake is bound to include this characteristic excellence. If an informing purpose is needed, no true artist can dispense with it. Otherwise art for art's sake is a contradiction in terms.

The critic I have quoted merely voices the lingering Puritan distrust of beauty as an end in itself, and so repudiates the conception of beauty as containing all the excellences of a work of art. He thinks of beauty as cut up into small snips and shreds of momentary sensations; as the sweet sound of melodious words and cadences; or as something abstract, pattern-like, imposed from without, — a Procrustes-bed of symmetry and proportion; or as a view of life Circe-like, insidious, a golden languor, made of "the selfish serenities of wild-wood and dream-palace." All these, apart or together, are thought of as the "beauty," at which the artist "for art's sake" aims, and to that is opposed the nobler informing purpose. But the truer view of beauty makes it simply the epitome of all which a work of art ought to be, and thus the only end and aim of every work of art. The beauty of literature receives into itself all the precepts of literature: there is no "ought" beyond it. And art for art's sake is but art conscious of its aim, the production of that all-embracing beauty.

What, then, is the beauty of literature? How may we know its characteristic excellences? It is strange how, in all serious discussion, to the confounding of some current ideas of criticism, we are thrown back, inevitably, on this concept of excellence! The most ardent of impressionists wakes up sooner or later to the idea that he has been talking values all his life. The excellences of literature! They must lie within the general formula for beauty, yet they must be conditioned by the possibilities of the special medium of literature. The general formula, abstract and metaphysical as it must be, may not be applied directly; for abstract

thought will fit only that art which can convey it;
hence the struggle of theorists with painting, music,
and architecture, and the failure of Hegel, for instance, to show how beauty as "the expression of
the Idea" resides in these arts. But if the general
formula is always translated relatively to the sense-
medium through which beauty must reach the
human being, it may be preserved, while yet affirm-
ing all the special demands of the particular art.
Beauty is a constant function of the varying medium. The end of Beauty is always the same, the
perfect moment of unity and self-completeness, of
repose in excitement. But this end is attained
by different means furnished by different media:
through vision and its accompanying activities;
through hearing and its accompanying activities;
and for literature, through hearing in the special
sense of communication by word. It is the nature
of this medium that we must further discover.

II

Now the word is nothing in itself; it is not
sound primarily, but thought. The word is but a
sign, a negligible quantity in human intercourse —
a counter in which the coins are ideas and emotions
— merely legal tender, of no value save in exchange. What we really experience in the sound
of a sentence, in the sight of a printed page, is a
complex sequence of visual and other images, ideas,

emotions, feelings, logical relations, swept along in
the stream of consciousness, — differing, indeed, in
certain ways from daily experience, but yet primarily of the web of life itself. The words in their
nuances, march, tempo, melody add certain elements
to this flood — hasten, retard, undulate, or calm it ;
but it is the *thought*, the understood experience,
that is the stuff of literature.

Words are first of all meanings, and meanings
are to be understood and lived through. We can
hardly even speak of the meaning of a word, but
rather of what it is, directly, in the mental state
that is called up by it. Every definition of a word
is but a feeble and distant approximation of the
unique flash of experience belonging to that word.
It is not the sound sensation nor the visual image
evoked by the word which counts, but the whole of
the mental experience, to which the word is but an
occasion and a cue. Therefore, since literature is
the art of words, it is the stream of thought itself
that we must consider as the material of literature.
In short, literature is the dialect of life — as Stevenson said ; it is by literature that the business of
life is carried on. Some one, however, may here
demur : visual signs, too, are the dialect of life.
We understand by what we see, and we live by
what we understand. The curve of a line, the crescendo of a note, serve also for wordless messages.
Why are not, then, painting and music the vehicles
of experience, and to be judged first as evocation of

life, and only afterward as sight and hearing ? This conceded, we are thrown back on that view of art as " the fixed quantity of imaginative thought supplemented by certain technical qualities, — of color in painting, of sound in music, of rhythmical words in poetry," from which it has been the one aim of the preceding arguments of this book to free us.

The holders of this view, however, ignore the history and significance of language. Our sight and hearing are given to us prior to our understanding or use of them. In a way, we submit to them — they are always with us. We dwell in them through passive states, through seasons of indifference ; moreover when we see to understand, we do not *see*, and when we hear to understand we do not hear. Only shreds of sensation, caught up in our flight from one action to another, serve as signals for the meanings which concern us. In proportion as action is prompt and effective, does the cue as such tend to disappear, until, in all matters of skill, piano-playing, fencing, billiard-playing, the sight or sound which serves as cue drops almost altogether out of consciousness. So far as it is vehicle of information, it is no longer sight or sound as such — interest has devoured it. But language came into being to supplement the lacks of sight and sound. It was created by ourselves, to embody all active outreaching mental experience, and it comes into particular existence to meet an insistent emergency

— a literally crying need. In short, it is *constituted* by meanings — its essence is communication. Sight and sound have a relatively independent existence, and may hence claim a realm of art that is largely independent of meanings. Not so the art of words, which can be but the art of meanings, of human experience alone.

And yet again, were the evocation of life the means and material of all art, that art in which the level of imaginative thought was low, the range of human experience narrow, would take a low place in the scale. What, then, of music and architecture? Inferior arts, they could not challenge comparison with the poignant, profound, all-embracing art of literature. But this is patently not the fact. There is no hierarchy of the arts. We may not rank St. Paul's Cathedral below " Paradise Lost." Yet if the material of all experience is the material of all art, they must not only be compared, but " Paradise Lost " must be admitted incomparably the greater. No — we may not admit that all the arts alike deal with the material of expression. The excellence of music and architecture, whatever it may be, cannot depend on this material. Yet by hypothesis it must be through the use of its material that the end of beauty is reached by every art. A picture has lines and masses and colors, wherewith to play with the faculty of vision, to weave a spell for the whole man. Beauty is the power to enchant him through the eye and all that waits upon it, into a moment of perfection. Literature has "all thoughts, all passions, all delights" — the treasury of life — to play with, to weave a spell for the whole man. Beauty in literature is the power to enchant him, through the mind and heart, across the dialect of life, into a moment of perfection.

III

The art of letters, then, is the art whose material is life itself. Such, indeed, is the implication of the approved theories of style. Words, phrases, sentences, chapters, are excellent in so far as they are identical with thought in all its shades of feeling. "Economy of attention," Spencer's familiar phrase for the philosophy of style, his explanation of even the most ornate and extravagant forms, is but another name for this desired lucidity of the medium. Pater, himself an artist in the overlaying of phrases, has the same teaching. " All the laws of good writing aim at a similar unity or identity of the mind in all the processes by which the word is associated to its import. The term is right, and has its essential beauty, when it becomes, in a manner, what it signifies, as with the names of simple sensations." [1] He quotes therewith De Maupassant on Flaubert: " Among all the expressions in the world, all forms and turns of expression, there is

[1] *Appreciations: An Essay on Style.*

but *one* — one form, one mode — to express what I want to say." And adds, " The one word for the one thing, the one thought, amid the multitude of words, terms, that might just do: the problem of style was there ! — the unique word, phrase, sentence, paragraph, essay, or song, absolutely proper to the single mental presentation or vision within." . . .

Thought in words is the matter of literature; and words exist but for thought, and get their excellence as thought; yet, as Flaubert says, the idea only exists by virtue of the form. The form, or the word, *is* the idea; that is, it carries along with it the fringe of suggestion which crystallizes the floating possibility in the stream of thought. A glance at the history of language shows how this must have been so. Words in their first formation were doubtless constituted by their imitative power. As Taine has said,[1] at the first they arose in contact with the objects; they imitated them by the grimaces of mouth and nose which accompanied their sound, by the roughness, smoothness, length, or shortness of this sound, by the rattle or whistle of the throat, by the inflation or contraction of the chest.

This primitive imitative power of the word survives in the so-called onomatopoetic words, which aim simply at reproducing the sounds of nature. A second order of imitation arises through the

[1] H. Taine, *La Fontaine et ses Fables*, p. 288.

associations of sensations. The different sensations, auditory, visual, olfactory, tactile, motor, and organic have common qualities, which they share with other more complex experiences; of form, as force or feebleness; of feeling, as harshness, sweetness, and so on. It is, indeed, another case of the form-qualities to which we recurred so often in the chapter on music. Clear and smooth vowels will give the impression of volatility and delicacy; open, broad ones of elevation or extension (airy, flee; large, far). The consonants which are hard to pronounce will give the impression of effort, of shock, of violence, of difficulty, of heaviness, — " the round squat turret, black as the fool's heart ; " those which are easy of pronunciation express ease, smoothness, fluidity, calm, lightness, (facile, suave, roulade) ; — " lucent syrops, tinct with cinnamon," a line like honey on the tongue, of which physical organ, indeed, one becomes, with the word " tinct," definitely conscious.

In fact, the main point to notice in the enumeration of the expressive qualities of sounds, is that it is the movement in utterance which characterizes them. That movement tends to reproduce itself in the hearer, and carries with it its feeling-tone of ease or difficulty, explosiveness or sweetness long drawn out. It is thus by a kind of sympathetic induction rather than by external imitation that these words of the second type become expressive.

Finally, the two moments may be combined, as in such a word as "roaring," which is directly imitative of a sound, and by the muscular activity it calls into play suggests the extended energy of the action itself.

The stage in which the word becomes a mere colorless, algebraic sign of object or process never occurs, practically, for in any case it has accumulated in its history and vicissitudes a fringe of suggestiveness, as a ship accumulates barnacles. "Words carry with them all the meanings they have worn," says Walter Raleigh in his "Essay on Style." "A slight technical implication, a faint tinge of archaism in the common turn of speech that you employ, and in a moment you have shaken off the mob that scours the rutted highway, and are addressing a select audience of ticket-holders with closed doors." Manifold may be the implications and suggestions of even a single letter. Thus a charming anonymous essay on the word "Grey." "Gray is a quiet color for daylight things, but there is a touch of difference, of romance, even, about things that are grey. Gray is a color for fur, and Quaker gowns, and breasts of doves, and a gray day, and a gentlewoman's hair; and horses must be gray. . . . Now grey is for eyes, the eyes of a witch, with green lights in them and much wickedness. Gray eyes would be as tender and yielding and true as blue ones; a coquette must have eyes of grey."

Words do not have meanings, they *are* meanings through their power of direct suggestion and induction. They may become what they signify. Nor is this power confined to words alone; on its possession by the phrase, sentence, or verse rests the whole theory of style. The short, sharp staccato, the bellowing turbulent, the swimming melodious circling sentence *are* truly what they mean, in their form as in the objective sense of their words. The sound-values of rhythm and pace have been in other chapters fully dwelt upon; the expressive power of breaks and variations is worth noting also. Of the irresistible significance of rhythm, even against content, we have an example amusingly commented on by Mr. G. K. Chesterton in his "Twelve Types." "He (Byron) may arraign existence on the most deadly charges, he may condemn it with the most desolating verdict, but he cannot alter the fact that on some walk in a spring morning when all the limbs are swinging and all the blood alive in the body, the lips may be caught repeating:

'Oh, there's not a joy the world can give like that it takes
    away,
When the glow of early youth declines in beauty's dull
    decay.'

That automatic recitation is the answer to the whole pessimism of Byron."

IV

Such, then, are some of the means by which language becomes identical with thought, and most truly the dialect of life. The genius will have ways, to which these briefly outlined ones will seem crude and obvious, but they will be none the less of the same nature. Shall we then conclude that the beauty of literature is here? that, in the words of Pater, from the essay I have quoted, "In that perfect justice (of the unique word) . . . omnipresent in good work, in function at every point, from single epithets to the rhythm of a whole book, lay the specific, indispensable, very intellectual beauty of literature, the possibility of which constitutes it a fine art."

In its last analysis, such a conception of literature amounts to the unimpeded intercourse of mind with mind. Literature would be a language which dispenses with gesture, facial expression, tone of voice; which is, in its halts, accelerations and retardations, emphases and concessions, the apotheosis of conversation. But this clearness, — in the sublime sense, including the ornate and the subtle, — this luminous lucidity, — is it not quite indeterminate? Clearness is said of a medium. *What* is it that shines through?

Were this clearness the beauty we are seeking, whatever in the world that wanted to get itself said, would, if it were perfectly said, become a final achievement of literature. All that the plain man looks for, we must think rightly, in poetry and prose, might be absent, and yet we should have to acknowledge its excellence. Let us then consider this quality by which the words become what they signify as the specific beauty rather of style than of literature; the mere refining of the gold from which the work of art has yet to be made. Language is the dialect of life; and the most perfect language can be no more than the most perfect truth of intercourse. It must then be through the treatment of life, or the sense of life itself, that we are somehow to attain the perfect moment of beauty.

The sense of life! In what meaning are these words to be taken? Not the completest sense of all, because the essence of life is in personal responsibility to a situation, and this is exactly what in our experience of literature disappears. First of all, then, before asking how the moment of beauty is to be attained, we must see how it is psychologically possible to have a sense of life that is yet purged of the will to live.

All experience of life is a complication of ideas, emotions, and attitudes or impulses to action in varying proportions. The sentiment of reality is constituted by our tendency to interfere, to " take a hand." Sometimes the stage of our consciousness is so fully occupied by the images of others that our own reaction is less vivid. Finally, all condi-

tions and possibilities of reaction may be so mini-
mized that the only attitude possible is our acceptance or rejection of a world in which such things
can be. What does it "matter" to me whether or
not "the old, unhappy, far-off things" really hap-
pened? The worlds of the Borgias, of Don Juan,
and of the Russian war stand on the same level of
reality. Aucassin and Nicolette are as near to me
as Abelard and Héloïse. For in relation to these
persons my impulse is *nil*. I submit to them, I
cannot change or help them; and because I have
no impulse to interfere, they are not vividly real to
me. And, in general, in so far as I am led to contemplate or to dwell on anything in idea, in so
far does my personal attitude tend to parallel this
impersonal one toward real persons temporally or
geographically out of reach.

Now in literature all conditions tend to the
enormous preponderance of the ideal element in
experience. My mind in reading is completely
filled with ideas of the appearance, ways, manners,
and situation of the people concerned. I leave
them a clear field. My emotions are enlisted only
as the inevitable fringe of association belonging to
vivid ideas — the ideas of their emotions. So far
as all the possibilities of understanding are fulfilled
for me, so far as I am in possession of all the conditions, so far do I "realize" the characters, but
realize them as ideas tinged with feeling.

Here there will be asseverations to the contrary.

What! feel no real emotion over Little Nell, or Colonel Newcome? no emotion in that great scene of passion and despair, the parting of Richard Feverel and Lucy, — a scene which none can read save with tight throat and burning eyes! Even so. It is not real emotion. You have the vivid ideas, so vivid that a fringe of emotional association accompanies them, as you might shudder remembering a bad dream. But the real emotion arises only from the real impulse, the real responsibility.

The sense of life that literature gives might be described as life in its aspect as idea. That this fact is the cause of the peace and painlessness of literature — since it is by his actions, as Aristotle says, that man is happy or the reverse — need not concern us here. For the beauty of literature, and our joy in it, lie not primarily in its lack of power to hurt us. The point is that literature gives none the less truly a sense of life because it happens to be one extreme aspect of life. The literary way is only one of the ways in which life can be met.

To give the sense of life perfectly — to create the illusion of life — is this, then, the beauty of literature? But we are seeking for the perfect moment of stimulation and repose. Why should the perfect illusion of life give this, any more than life itself does? So the " vision " of a picture might be intensely clear, and yet the picture itself unbeautiful. Such a complete " sense of life," such clear " vision," would show the artist's mastery of technique, but not his power to create beauty. In the art of literature, as in the art of painting, the normal function is but the first condition, the state of perfection is the end at which to aim.

It is just this distinction that we can properly make between the characteristic or typical in the sense of differentiated, and the great or excellent in literature. In the theory of some writers, perfect fidelity to the type is the only originality. To paint the Russian peasant or the French bourgeois as he is, to catch the exact shade of exquisite soullessness in Oriental loves, to reproduce the Berserker rage or the dull horror of battle, is indeed to give the perfect sense of life. But the perfect, or the complete, sense of life is not the moment of perfect life.

Yet to this assertion two answers might be made. The authors of " Bel-Ami," or " Madame Chrysanthème," or " The Triumph of Death," might claim to be saved by their form. The march of events, the rounding climax, the crystal-clear unity of the finished work, they might say, gives the indispensable union, for the perfect moment of stimulation and repose. No syllable in the slow unfolding of exquisite cadences but is supremely placed from the first page to the last. As note calls to note, so thought calls to thought, and feeling to feeling, and the last word is an answer to the first of the inevitable procession. A writer's *donnée*, they

would say, is his own. The reader may only beg —
Make me something fine after your own fashion!

And they would have to be acknowledged partly
in the right. In that inevitable unity of form there
is indeed a necessary element of the perfect moment; but it is not a perfect unity. For the matter
of their art should be, in the last analysis, life itself;
and the unity of life itself, the one basic unity of
all, they have missed. It is a hollow sphere they
present, and nothing solid. Henry James has spent
the whole of a remarkable essay on D'Annunzio's
creations in determining the meaning of "the fact
that their total beauty somehow extraordinarily
fails to march with their beauty of parts, and that
something is all the while at work undermining
that bulwark against ugliness which it is their obvious theory of their own office to throw up." The
secret is, he avers, that the themes, the "anecdotes,"
could find their extension and consummation only
in the rest of life. Shut out, as they are, from the
rest of life, shut out from all fruition and assimilation, and so from all hope of dignity, they lose
absolutely their power to sway us.

It might be simpler to say that these works lack
the first beauty which literature as the dialect of
life can have — they lack the repose of centrality;
they have no identity with the meaning of life as a
whole. It could not be said of them, as Bagehot
said of Shakespeare: "He puts things together, he
refers things to a principle; rather, they group

themselves in his intelligence insensibly around a principle; . . . a cool oneness, a poised personality, pervades him." But in these men there is no cool oneness, no reasonable soul, and so they miss the central unity of life, which can give unity to literature. Even the apparent structural unity fails when looked at closely; the actions of the characters are seen to be mechanical — their meaning is not inevitable.

The second answer to our assertion that the "sense of life" is not the beauty of literature might call attention to the fact that *sense* of life may be taken as understanding of life. A complete sense of life must include the conditions of life, and the conditions of life involve this very "energetic identity" on which we have insisted. And this contention we must admit. So long as the sense of life is taken as the illusion of life, our words hold good. But if to that is added understanding of life, the door is open to the profoundest excellences of literature. Henry James has glimpsed this truth in saying that no good novel will ever proceed from a superficial mind. Stevenson has gone further. "But the truth is when books are conceived under a great stress, with a soul of ninefold power, nine times heated and electrified by effort, the conditions of our being are seized with such an ample grasp, that even should the main design be trivial or base, some truth and beauty cannot fail to be expressed."

V

The conditions of our being! If we accept, affirm, profoundly rest in what is presented to us, we have the first condition of that repose which is the essence of the æsthetic experience. And from this highest demand can be viewed the hierarchy of the lesser perfections which go to make up the "perfect moment" of literature. Instead of reaching this point by successive eliminations, we might indeed have reached it in one stride. The perfect moment across the dialect of life, the moment of perfect life, must be in truth that in which we touch the confines of our being, look upon our world, all in all, as revealed in some great moment, and see that it is good — that we grasp it, possess it, that it is akin to us, that it is identical with our deepest wills. The work that grasps the conditions of our being gives ourselves back to us completed.

In the conditions of our being in a less profound sense may be found the further means to the perfect moment. Thus the progress of events, the development of feelings, must be in harmony with our natural processes. The development, the rise, complication, expectation, gratification, the suspense, climax, and drop of the great novel, correspond to the natural functioning of our mental processes. It is an experience that we seek, multiplied, perfected, expanded — the life moment of a man greater than we. This, too, is the ultimate meaning of the demands of style. Lucidity, indeed, there must be, — identity with the thought ; but besides the value of the thought in its approximation to the conditions of our being, we seek the vividness of that thought, — the perfect moment of apprehension, as well as of experience. It is the beauty of style to be lucid ; but the beauty of lucidity is to reinforce the springs of thought.

Even to the minor elements of style, the tone-coloring, the rhythm, the melody, — the essence of beauty, that is, of the perfect moment, is given by the perfecting of the experience. The beauty of liquids is their ease and happiness of utterance. The beauty of rhythm is its aiding and compelling power, on utterance and thought. There is a sensuous pleasure in a great style ; we love to mouth it, for it is made to mouth. As Flaubert says somewhat brutally, " Je ne sais qu'une phrase est bonne qu'après l'avoir fait passer par mon gueuloir."

In the end it might be said that literature gives us the moment of perfection, and is thus possessed of beauty, when it reveals ourselves to ourselves in a better world of experience ; in the conditions of our moral being, in the conditions of our thought processes, in the conditions of our utterance and our breathing ; — all these, concentric circles, in which the centre of repose is given by the underlying identity of ourselves with this world. Because it goes to the roots of experience, and seeks to give the conditions of our being as they really are, literature may be truly called a criticism of life. Yet the end of literature is not the criticism of life ; rather the appreciation of life — the full savour of life in its entirety. The final definition of literature is the art of experience.

VI

But then literature would give only the perfect moments of existence, would ignore the tragedies, ironies, pettiness of life! Such an interpretation is a quite mistaken one. As the great painting uses the vivid reproduction of an ugly face, a squalid hovel, to create a beautiful picture, beautiful because all the conditions of seeing are made to contribute to our being made whole in seeing ; so great literature can attain through any given set of facts to the deeper harmony of life, can touch the one poised, unconquerable soul, and can reinforce the moment of self-completeness by every parallel device of stimulation and concentration. And because it is most often in the tragedies that the conditions of our being are laid bare, and the strings which reverberate to the emotions most easily played upon, it is likely that the greatest books of all will be the tragedies themselves. The art of experience needs contrasts no less than does the visual or auditory art.

This beauty of literature, because it is a hierarchy of beauties more and less essential, exists in all varieties and in all shades. If the old comparison and contrast of idealism and realism is referred to here, it is because that ancient controversy seems not even yet entirely outworn. If realism means close observation of facts and neglect of ideas, and idealism, neglect of prosaic facts and devotion to ideas, then we must admit that realism and idealism are the names of two defective types. Strictly speaking, whatever goes deep enough to the truth of things, gets nearer reality, is realism; yet to get nearer reality is to attain true ideas, and that is idealism too. The great work of literature is realistic because it does not lose sight of the ideal. Our popular use of idealistic refers, indeed, to the world seen through rose-colored glasses; but for that possible variety of literary effort it is better to use the word Romance. Romance is the world of our youthful dreams of things, not as they do happen, or as in our nobler moments we will them to happen, but as, without any special deeper meaning, we should wish them to happen. That is the world of the gold-haired maiden, " the lover with the red-roan steed of steeds," the purse of Fortunatus, the treasure-trove, the villain confronted with his guilt. " Never the time and the place and the loved one all together! " But in Romance they come together. The total depravity of inanimate things has become the stars in their courses fighting for us. Stevenson calls it the poetry of circumstance — for the dreams of youth

are properly healthy and material. The salvage
from the wreck in "Robinson Crusoe," he tells
us, satisfies the mind like things to eat. Romance
gives us the perfect moment of the material and
human — with the divine left out.

It has sometimes been made a reproach to critics
— more often, I fear, by those who hold, like myself, that beauty and excellence in art are identical — that they discourse too little of form in
literature, and too much of content. But all our
taking thought will have been vain, if it is not
now patent that the first beauty of literature is,
and must be, its identity with the central flame of
life, — the primal conditions of our being. Thus it
is that the critic is justified in asking first of all,
How does this man look on life? Has he revealed
a new — or better — the eternal old meaning? The
Weltanschauung is the critic's first consideration,
and after that he may properly take up that secondary grasp of the conditions of our being in mental
processes, revealed in the structure, march of incidents, suspense, and climaxes, and the beauty or
idiosyncracy of style. It is then literally false that
it does not matter what a man says, but only how
he says it. What he says is all that matters, for it
will not be great thought without some greatness in
the saying. Art for art's sake in literature is then
art for life's sake, and the "informing purpose," in
so far as that means the vision of our deepest selves,
is its first condition.

And because the Beauty of Literature is constituted by its quality as life itself, we may defer detailed consideration of the species and varieties of
literature. Prose and poetry, drama and novel,
have each their own special excellences springing
from the respective situations they had, and have,
to meet. Yet these but add elements to the one
great power they all must have as literature, —
the power to give the perfect experience of life in
its fullness and vividness, and in its identity with
the central meanings of existence, — unity and self-
completeness together, — in a form which offers to
our mental functions the perfect moment of stimulation and repose.

VII

THE NATURE OF THE EMO-
TIONS OF THE DRAMA

VII

THE NATURE OF THE EMOTIONS OF THE DRAMA

I

THAT psychologist who, writing on the problems of dramatic art, called his brochure "The Dispute over Tragedy," gave the right name to a singular situation. Of all the riddles of æsthetic experience, none has been so early propounded, so indefatigably attempted, so variously and unsatisfactorily solved, as this. What is dramatic? What constitutes a tragedy? How can we take pleasure in painful experiences? These questions are like Banquo's ghost, and will not down.

The ingenious Bernays has said that it was all the fault of Aristotle. The last phrase of the famous definition in the "Poetics," which should relate the nature, end, and aim of tragedy, is left, in his works as we have them, probably through the suppression or loss of context, without elucidating commentary. And the writers on tragedy have ever since so striven to guess his meaning, and to make their answers square with contemporary drama, that they have given comparatively slight attention to the immediate, unbiased investigation of the phe-

nomenon itself. Aristotle's definition is as follows : [1]
" Tragedy, then, is an imitation of an action that
is serious, complete, and of a certain magnitude ;
in language embellished with each kind of artistic
ornament, the several kinds being found in separate parts of the play : in the form of action, not
of narrative ; through pity and fear effecting the
proper purgation of these emotions." In what follows, he takes up and explains this definition, phrase
by phrase, until the very last. What is meant by
the Purgation (Katharsis) through pity and fear ?
It is at least what tragedy " effects," and is thus
evidently the function of tragedy. But a thing is
determined, constructed, judged, according to its
function ; the function is, so to speak, its genetic
formula. With a clear view of that, the rest of
the definition could conceivably have been constructed without further explanation ; without it,
the key to the whole fails. " Purgation of these
emotions ;" did it mean purification of the emotions,
or purgation of the soul *from* the emotions ? And
what emotions ? Pity and fear, or " these and such-
like," thus including all emotions that tragedy could
bring to expression ?

Our knowledge of the severely moral bent of the
explicit art criticism of the Greeks has inclined
many to accept the first interpretation ; and modern interests impel in the same direction. It is natural to think of the generally elevating and soften-

[1] S. H. Butcher, *Aristotle's Theory of Poetry and Fine Art*, 1895.

ing effects of great art as a kind of moral clarifying, and the question how this should be effected just by pity and fear was not pressed. So Lessing in the " Hamburgische Dramaturgie " takes Katharsis as the conversion of the emotions in general into virtuous dispositions.

Before we ask ourselves seriously how far this represents our experience of the drama, we must question its fidelity to the thought of Aristotle ; and that question seems to have received a final answer in the exhaustive discussion of Bernays.[1] Without going into his arguments, suffice it to say that Aristotle, scientist and physician's son as he was, had in mind in using this striking metaphor of the Katharsis of the emotions, a perfectly definite procedure, familiar in the treatment, by exciting music, of persons overcome by the ecstasy or " enthusiasm " characteristic of certain religious rites. Bernays quotes Milton's preface to " Samson Agonistes : " " Tragedy is said by Aristotle to be of power, by raising pity and fear, or terror, to purge the mind of those and such like passions ; that is, to temper and reduce them to just measure with a kind of delight, stirred by reading or seeing those passions well imitated. Nor is Nature wanting in her own effects to make good his assertion ; for so in physic, things of melancholic hue and quality are used against melancholy, sour against sour,

[1] *Zwei Adhandlungen uber d. Aristotelische Theorie d. Drama,* 1880.

salt to remove salt humours," adding " the homœo-
pathic comparison shows how near he was to the
correct notion." Bernays concludes that by Katharsis is denoted the " alleviating discharge " of the
emotions themselves. In other words, pity and fear
are bad, and it is a good thing to get rid of them
in a harmless way, as it is better to be vaccinated
than to have small pox.

Now this alleviating discharge is pleasurable
($\mu\epsilon\theta'$ $\dot{\eta}\delta o\nu\hat{\eta}s$), and the pleasure seems, from allied
passages, to arise not in the accomplished relief from
oppression, but in the process itself. This becomes
intelligible from the point of view of Aristotle's
definition of pleasure as an ecstatic condition of
the soul. For every emotion contains, according to
Aristotle, be it ever so painful, an ecstatic, and
hence a pleasurable element ; so that the excitement
of pity and fear in the ecstatic degree would effect,
at the same time with an alleviating discharge, a
pleasure also. Pity and fear are aroused to be al-
layed, and to give pleasure in the arousing and the
relief.

Such, approximately, is Aristotle's view of the
Tragic Emotion, or Katharsis. Is it also our own ?
To clear the field for this inquiry, it will be well
first of all to insist on a distinction which is mostly
discounted in significance because taken for
granted. We speak of Aristotle's Katharsis as the
Tragic Emotion, forgetting that to-day Tragedy
and the Tragic are no longer identical. Aristotle

conceives himself to be dealing with the peculiar emotion aroused by a certain dramatic form, the name of which has nothing to do with its content. For Tragedy is literally *goat-song,* perhaps from the goat-skins worn by the first performers of tragedy disguised as satyrs. Since then we have borrowed the name of that dramatic form to apply to events which have the same type or issue as in that form. In popular speech to-day the word tragic attaches itself rather to the catastrophe than to the struggle, and therefore, I cannot but think, modern discussion of " the tragic " is wrong in attempting to combine the Aristotelian and the modern shades of meaning, and to embody them both in a single definition. Aristotle is dealing with the whole effect of the dramatic representation of what we should call a tragic occurrence. It is really the theory of the dramatic experience and not of the tragic, in our sense, which occupies him. Therefore, as I say, we must not assume, with many modern critics, that an analysis of the tragic in experience will solve the problem of the Katharsis. Our " tragic event," it is true, is of the kind which dramatically treated helped to bring about this peculiar effect. But the question of Aristotle and our problem of Katharsis is the problem of the emotion aroused by the Tragic Drama. What, then, is the nature of dramatic emotion ?

II

The analogy of Aristotle's conception of the emotion of tragedy with certain modern views is evident. To feel pain is to live intensely, it is said; to be absorbed in great, even though overwhelming, events is to make us realize our own pulsing life. The criticism to be made on this theory is, however, no less simple: it consists merely in denying the fact. It does not give us pleasure to have painful emotions or to see other people's sorrows, in spite of the remains of the "*gorille féroce*" in us, to which Taine and M. Faguet attribute this imputed pleasure. And if we feel pleasure, excitement, elevation in the representation of the tragic, it must be due to some other element in the experience than the mere self-realization involved in suffering. It is indeed our first impulse to say that the painful quality vanishes when the exciting events are known to be unreal; pity and fear are painful because too intense, and in the drama are just sufficiently moderated. The rejoinder is easy, that pity and fear are never anything but painful down to the vanishing point. The slight pity for a child's bruised finger is not more pleasurable because less keen; while our feeling, whatever it is, for Ophelia or Gretchen, becomes more pleasurable in proportion to its intensity.

It is clear that the matter is not so simple as

Aristotle's psychology would make it. Pity and fear do not in themselves produce pleasure, relief, and repose. These emotions as aroused by tragedy are either not what we know as pity and fear in real life, or the manner of their undergoing brings in an entirely new element, on which Aristotle has not touched. In some way or other the pity and fear of tragedy are not like the pity and fear of real life, and in this distinction lies the whole mystery of the dramatic Katharsis.

But there is an extension of Aristotle's theory, lineally descended from that of Lessing, which professes to elucidate this difference and must be taken account of, inasmuch as it represents the modern popular view. Professor Butcher, in his edition of the "Poetics," concludes, on the basis of a reference in the "Politics" implying that the Katharsis of enthusiasm is not identical with the Katharsis of pity and fear, that the word is to be taken less literally, as an expulsion of the morbid elements in the emotions, — and these he takes to be the selfish elements which cling to them in real life. Thus "the spectator, who is brought face to face with grander sufferings than his own, experiences a sympathetic ecstasy, a lifting out of himself. It is precisely in this transport of feeling, which carries a man outside his individual self, that the distinctive tragic pleasure resides. Pity and fear are purged of the impure element which clings to them in life. In the glow of tragic excitement these feelings are so transformed that the net result is a noble emotional satisfaction."

In spite of our feeling that the literal and naïve reading of the analogy was probably after all nearer Aristotle's meaning, we may accept the words of Professor Butcher as its modern formulation. They sound, indeed, all but a truism: yet they are seen on examination to glide lightly over some psychological difficulties. Firstly, the step is a long one from the pity and fear felt by the Greek toward or about the actors, to a sharing of their emotion. The one is a definite external relation, limited to two emotions; the other, the "sympathetic ecstasy," opens the door to all conceivable emotions, and needs at least to be justified. But, secondly, even suppose the step taken; suppose the "sympathetic imitation" conceded as a fact: the objections to Aristotle's interpretation are equally applicable to this. Why should this "transport of sympathetic feeling" not take the form of a transport of pain? Why should the net result be "a noble emotional satisfaction?" If pity and fear remain pity and fear, whether selfish or unselfish, it doth not yet appear why they are emotionally satisfactory. The "so transformed" of the passage quoted assumes the point at issue and begs the question. That is, if this transformation of feeling does indeed take place, there is at least nothing in the nature of the situation, as yet explained, to account for it. But explanation there must be. To this, the lost passage on the Katharsis must have been devoted ; this, every thorough-going study of the theory of the drama must make an indispensable preliminary. What there is in the nature of tragic art capable of transforming painful to pleasurable emotion must be made clear. Before we can accept Professor Butcher's view of the function of Tragedy, its possibility as a psychological experience must be demonstrated. For the immediately pleasurable æsthetic effect of Tragedy, a certain kind of pity and fear, operating in a special way, are required. It must be thus only in the peculiar character of the emotions aroused that the distinctive nature of the tragic experience consists. What is this peculiar character ?

III

A necessary step to the explanation of our pleasure in supposedly painful emotions is to make clear how we can feel any emotion at all in watching what we know to be unreal, and to show how this emotion is sympathetic, that is, imitative, rather than of an objective reference. In brief, why do we feel *with*, rather than toward or about, the actors ?

The answer to this question requires a reference to the current theory of emotion. According to modern psychologists, emotion is constituted by the instinctive response to a situation ; it is the feeling accompanying very complicated physical reactions, which have their roots in actions once useful in the history of mankind. Thus the familiar "expression" of anger, the flushed face, dilated nostril, clenched fist, are remains or marks of reactions serviceable in mortal combat. But these, the "coarser" bodily changes proper to anger, are accompanied by numberless organic reactions, the "feel" of all of which together is an indispensable element of the emotion of anger. The point to be noted in all this is that these reactions are *actions*, called up by something with which we literally *have to do*.

A person involved in real experience does not reproduce the emotions about him, for in real life he must respond to the situation, take an attitude of help, consolation, warning; and the character of these reactions determines for him an emotion of his own. Even though he really do nothing, the multitudinous minor impulses to action going to make up his attitude appreciably interfere with the reproduction of the reactions of the object of his interest. In an exactly opposite way the artificial conditions of the spectator at a play, which reinforce the vivid reproduction of ideas, and check action, stifle those emotions directed toward the players, the objective emotions of which we have spoken. The spectator is completely cut off from all possibilities of influence on events. Between his world and that across the footlights an inexpressible gulf is fixed. He cannot take an "attitude," he can have nothing to do in this *galère*. Since he may not act, even those beginnings of action which make the basis of emotion are inhibited in him. The spectator at a play experiences much more clearly and sharply than the sympathetic observer; only the proportions of his mental contents are different. This, I say, accounts for the absence of the real pity and fear, which were supposed to be directed toward the persons in the play. But so far as yet appears there is every reason to expect the sympathetic reproduction of the emotions of the persons themselves.

Let us briefly recall the situation. The house is darkened and quiet; all lines converge to the stage, which is brightly lighted, and heightened in visual effect by every device known to art. The onlooker's mind is emptied of its content; all feeling of self is pushed down to its very lowest level. He has before him a situation which he understands through sight and hearing, and in which he follows the action not only by comprehension, but by instinctive imitation. This is the great vehicle of suggestion. We cannot see tears rise without moisture in our own eyes; we reproduce a yawn even against our will; the sudden or the regular movement of a companion we are forced to follow, at least incipiently. Now the expression which we imitate brings up in us to a certain extent the whole complex of ideas and feeling-tones belonging to that expression. Moreover, the more closely we attend to it, the more explicitly do we imitate it, by an evident psychological principle. Thus in the artificially contrived situation of the spectator at a play, he is forced, not only to understand intellectually, but also to *follow*, quite literally, the emotional movements of the actors. The process of understanding, raised to the highest pitch, involves by its very nature also reproduction of what is understood. The complex of the ideas and associations of the persons of the play is ideally reproduced. Are not the organic reactions belonging to these set up too? — not directly, in response to a situation in which the spectator may act, but indirectly, by reproduction of the mental contents of one who may act, the person of the drama. The final answer to this question contains, to my mind, the whole kernel of the dramatic mystery, and the starting-point for an æsthetic theory of tragedy.

IV

Every play contains at least two actors. The suggestion of states of mind does not come from the hero alone, but is given by two persons, or groups of persons, at once. These persons are, normally, in conflict. Othello menaces, Desdemona shrinks ; Nora asserts her right, Hilmar his claim ; L'Aiglon vaunts his inherited personality, Metternich — holds the candle to the mirror ! But what of the spectator ? He cannot at once shrink and menace, assert and deny, as the conditions of sympathetic reproduction would seem to demand. Real emotion implies a definite set of reactions of the nature of movements; and two opposed movements cannot take place at the same time. Ideas, however, can dwell together in amity. The spectator has a vivid picture of Othello and Desdemona together; but his reactions have neutralized each other, and his emotions, lacking their organic conditions, are in abeyance.

This is the typical dramatic moment, for it is the one which is alone characteristic of the drama. Only in the simultaneous realization of two opposing forces is the full mutual checking of emotional impulses possible, and it is only in this simultaneous realization that the drama differs from all other forms of art. When the two antagonistic purposes are actually presented to the onlooker in the same moment of time, then alone can be felt the vividness of realization, the tension of conflict, the balance of emotion, the " alleviation " of the true Katharsis !

But what is this ? No emotion after all, when the very traditional test of our enjoyment of a play is the amount of feeling it arouses ! — when hearts beat, hands clench, tears flow ! Emotion there is, it may not be denied ; but not the sympathetic emotions of the traditional theory.

What emotion? The mutual checking of impulses issues in a balance, a tension, a conflict which is yet a bond; and this it is which is the clue to the excitement or exaltation which in the dramatic experience usurps the place of definite feeling. We have met this phenomenon before. Æsthetic emotion in general, we have heard, consists just in the union of a kind of stimulation or enhanced life, with repose; a heightening of the vital energies unaccompanied by any tendency to movement, — in short, that gathering of forces which we connect with action, and which is felt the more because action is checked. Just such a repose through equilibrium of impulses is given by the dramatic conflict. Introspection makes assurance doubly sure. The tense exaltation of the typical æsthetic experience, undirected, unlimited, pure of personal or particular reference, is reproduced in this nameless ecstasy of the tragic drama. The mysterious Katharsis, the emotion of tragedy, is, then, a special type of the unique æsthetic emotion.

And it is the singular peculiar characteristic of the drama — the face to face confrontation of forces — which furnishes these conditions. As we might have foreseen, the peculiar Katharsis, or pleasurable disappearance or alleviation of emotion in tragedy, is based on just those elements in which the drama differs from other forms of art. Confrontation, and not action, as the dramatic principle, is the important deduction from our theory; — is, indeed, but the objective aspect of it.

The view of confrontation as the dramatic principle is confirmed by dramatic literature. We emphasize in our study of Greek plays their sim-

plicity of plot, their absence of intrigue, their
sculptural, bas-relief quality. The Greek drama
makes of a poem a *crisis,* says M. Faguet. A
tragedy is a well-composed group, a fine contrast,
a beautiful effect of imposing symmetry — as in
the "Antigone," "on one side civil law in all its
blind rigor, on the other moral law in all its splen-
dor." The only element in common with the modern type is found in the conflict of wills. Could
such a play as the "Suppliants" of Euripides find
any æsthetic justification, save that it has the one
dramatic essential — confrontation, balance of emotions? The very scenes of short speeches, of ob-
jurgation or sententious repartee, which cannot but
have for us an element of the grotesque, must have
been as pleasing as they were to the Greek audience, from the fact that they brought to sharpest
vision the confrontation of the two antagonists.
The mediæval drama, which has become popularly
known in "Everyman," is nothing but a succession of duels, material or spiritual. It is indeed the
two profiles confronting one another, our sympathy
balanced, and suspended, as it were, between them,
which characterize our recollections of this whole
great field. The modern critics and comparers of
English and French drama are fond of contrasting
the full, rich, even prodigal characterization, rhe-
torical and lyrical beauty of the Shakespearean
drama with the cold, clear, logical, but resistless
movement of the French. Yet the contrast is not

quite that between characterization and form; the essential form is common to both. In the first place, Elizabethan drama was platform drama — that is, by the testimony of contemporaries, little concerned with anything but the succession of more or less unconnected scenes between two or three persons. And we see clearly that the great dramatic power of " Hamlet," for instance, must lie, not in the movement of a wavering purpose, but in the separate scenes of his struggle, each one wonderfully rich, vivid, balanced, but almost a unit in itself. On the theory that the true dramatic form is logical progress, dramatic — as contrasted with literary — power would have to be denied to " Hamlet." The æsthetic meaning of " Lear " is not in the terrible retribution of pride and self-will, but in the cruel confrontation of father and daughters.

This is no less true of the first great French plays. It is certainly not the resistless movement of the intrigue which makes the " Misanthrope," " Tartufe," the " Précieuses Ridicules," masterpieces of comedy as well as of literature. Their dramatic value lies in their piquancy of confrontation. The tug-of-war between Alceste and Célimène, between Rodrigue and Chimène in " Le Cid," is what we think of as dramatic ; and it is this same element which is found as well in the complicated and overflowing English plays. And in modern French drama, for all its " logic," the dominating factor is the " scène à faire," — what I have called the scene of confrontation. The notoriously successful scene in the English drama of to-day, the duel of Sophy and Lord Quex — tolerably empty of real feeling or significance though it is — becomes successful merely through the consummate handling of the face-to-face element. Only by admitting this æsthetic moment of arrest can we allow dramatic value to such a play as " Les Affaires sont les Affaires " — a truly static drama. The hero of this is, in the words of a reviewer, " essentially the same force in magnitude and direction from the rise to the fall of the curtain. It does not move; it is we who are taken around it so that we may see its various facets. It is not moulded by the successive incidents of the play, but only disclosed by them; *sibi constat.*" Yet we cannot deny to the play dramatic power; and the reason for this is, as I believe, because it does, after all, possess the dramatic essential — not action, but tension.

V

It will be demanded, however, what place there is then for a temporal factor, if the typical dramatic experience depends upon the great scene? It cannot be denied that the drama is a work of art developed in time, like music and poetry. It comes to a climax and a resolution; it evolves its harmonies like the symphony, in irrevocable order.

We cannot afford to neglect, in such an æsthetic analysis, what is an undoubted element in dramatic effect, the so-called inevitable march of events. In answer to this objection we may hold that the temporal factor is a corollary of the primary demand for confrontation. It is necessary that the confrontation or conflict should be vividly imagined, with all possible associative reinforcements — that it should be brought up to the turn of the screw, as it were. For this, then, motivation is absolutely necessary. An attitude is only clearly " realized " when it is made to seem inevitable. It takes complete possession of our minds only when it inhibits all other possibilities. At any given scene, the power of a part to reproduce itself in us is measured by the convincing quality given it by motivation, and for this there must be a full body of associations to draw on, to round out and complete understanding. The villain of the play is, for instance, less completely " suggested " to us, because our associations are supposedly less rich for such characters ; as a beggar hypnotized and made to feel himself a king has meagre mental equipment for the part. Now, this inner possession can come about only through the compelling force of a long course of preparation. In providing such an accumulation of impulses, none was greater than the younger Dumas — and none had to be greater ! To make his audience accept — that is, identify itself with — the action of the hero in " Denise,"

or the mother's decision in " Les Idées de Mme.
Aubray," so subversive of general social feeling, and
thereby to experience fully the great dramatic moment 'in each play, there had to go the effect of
innumerable small impulses. And to realize some
situations is even beyond the scope of a play's development. It is an acute remark of Mr. G. K.
Chesterton's, that many plays nowadays turn on
problems of marriage : which subject is one for
slow years of adjustment, patience, adaptation, en-
deavor ; while the drama requires quick decisions,
bouleversements, etc., and would do wisely to confine itself to fields in which such bouleversements
can be made credible. At any rate, motivation is
desirable for the dramatic confrontation, and time
— the working-out — is an essential condition of
motivation. To make the dramatic conflict ever
sharper and deeper, until it either melts into harmony, or ceases through the destruction of one
element, is the whole duty of the development,
and makes it necessary. That development is temporal, is, dramatically, only a device for damming
the flood that it may break at last with greater
force.

This, too, is an answer to the objection that if
confrontation is the dramatic essential, bare opposition, because the clearest confrontation, would be
the greatest drama, and the " Suppliants " of Euripides be indeed an example of it. Bare opposition
is never real confrontation in our sense, for that

must be an arrest, a mutual antagonism of all impulses of soul and sense. It must possess the whole man. It needs to take in " all thoughts, all passions, all delights," to be complete, and the measure of its completeness is the measure of its æsthetic value.

In the same way, the demand for profound truth and significance in the drama is clearly to be reached from the purely dramatic need. Inner " possession," the condition for our dramatic tension, depends not alone on the cumulation of suggestions — suggestion in its, so to speak, quantitative aspect. The attitude of a character must be necessary in itself: that is, it must be true to the great and general laws of life. If it is fundamentally false, even with the longest and completest preparation, it rings hollow. We cannot completely enter into it. Thus we see that the one central requirement, the dramatic germ, leads to the most far-reaching demands for logic, sanity, and morality in the ideas of a play.

This should not be interpreted as exhausting the æsthetic value of logic and morality in the drama. The drama is a species of literature: and these qualities, apart from the fact that they are necessary to the full dramatic moment, have also an æsthetic effect proper to themselves. Thus the development has the beauty which lies in a necessary progress; but this beauty is common to the epic, the novel, and the symphony, while the unity given by the confrontation and tension of simultaneous forces belongs to the drama alone. It is therefore development as serving the dramatic end that I have deduced.

Yet we may well recall here the other aspect of the experience. Analogous to the pleasure in rhythm and in music, in which the awaited beat or tone slips, as it were, into a place already prepared for it, with the satisfaction of harmonious nervous adjustment, is the pleasure in an inevitable and irrevocable progress. For it is not felt as inevitable unless the whole crystallization of the situation makes such, and only such, an action or thought necessary at a certain point in the structure, makes it to a certain extent anticipated, and so recognized with acclaim on its appearance. We will an event in anticipating and accepting it; and we realize it as it comes. Nothing more is to be found in the psychological analysis of the will itself — theoretically, the two states are nearly identical. Thus this continual anticipation and " coming true " takes on the feeling-tone of all volition; and so in music, as I have shown at length, and in drama, and to a degree in all forms of literature, we have the illusion of the triumphant will. This is the secret of that creative joy felt by the spectator at a drama, which has been so often noted. It is this illusion of the triumphant will, too, which enters largely into our acceptance of the tragic end. Much has been said, in the " dispute over tragedy,"

of the so-called " Resignation " of the tragic hero,
and of the audience in relation to his fate.   But I
believe that these writers are wrong in connecting
this resignation primarily with a moral attitude.
What is foreseen as perfectly inevitable, is sufficiently " accepted " in the psychological sense —
that is, vividly imagined and awaited, — to contribute to this illusion of volition.   Hence arise,
for the catastrophe of drama, that exaltation and
stern joy which are indissolubly connected with the
experience of will in real life.

VI

We have spoken of the dramatic, and have desired to show that its peculiar æsthetic experience
arises out of the tension or balance of emotion in
the confrontation of opposing forces.   If this is a
fruitful theory, it should throw light on the distinction between the different forms of the drama,
and on the principal issues of that " Dispute over
Tragedy " which is always with us.

The possible results of a meeting of two forces
are these.   Both forces, or one force, may be destroyed ; or, short of destruction, the two may melt
into harmony, or one may give way before the
other.   I think it may be said that these alterna-
tives represent the distinctions of Tragedy and
Comedy.   When two aims are absolutely irreconcilable, and when the forces tending to them are

important, — that is, powerful, — there must be somewhere destruction, and we have tragedy. When they are reconcilable, if they are important, we have serious comedy; when not important, or not envisaged as important, we have light comedy. Thus Tragedy and Comedy are closely related, — more closely than we are prone to think. In the words of the late Professor Everett, in " Poetry, Comedy, and Duty:" "The tragic is, like the comic, simply the incongruous. The great Tragedy of Nature, which is called the Struggle for Existence, results simply from a greater or less incongruousness between any form of life and its surroundings. . . . The comic is found in an incongruous relation considered merely as to its *form*, while the tragic is found in an incongruous relation taken as to its reality." For this word incongruity I would substitute collision or conflict. When there is no way out, we have Tragedy; when there is a way out, we have Comedy. And when things are taken superficially enough, there always is a way out, for we can at least always agree to disagree. In any case, the end of the conflict is a period, repose, unity. This seems to be borne out by immediate introspection. The feelings with which we come from a great tragedy or a great comedy are indeed almost identical. The excitement, tension, sunk into repose, are common to both; the satisfaction with a good ending is strangely paralleled by our resignation to a bad one, — significant of

our real indifference to the fact, so long as the
Æsthetic Unity is reached.

In George Meredith's wonderful little essay on
the Comic Spirit, this view is rather remarkably
confirmed. He has defined Comedy as the contrast
of the middle way, the way of common sense, with
our human vagaries, " Comme un point fixe fait
remarquer l'emportement des autres." Comedy, he
says, teaches the world to understand what ails it.
. . . " Comedy is the fountain of sound sense," and
again, " the use of the true comedy is to awaken
thoughtful laughter." " Men's future upon earth
does not attract it ; their honesty and shapeliness
in the present does ; and whenever they wax out
of proportion, overblown, affected, pretentious,
bombastical, hypocritical, pedantic, fantastically
delicate ; whenever it sees them self-deceived or
hoodwinked, given to run riot in idolatries, drifting
into vanities, congregating in absurdities, planning
shortsightedly, plotting dementedly ; whenever they
are at variance with their professions, and violate
the unwritten but perceptible laws binding them
in consideration one to another ; whenever they
offend sound reason, fair justice ; are false in
humility or moved with conceit, individually or in
the bulk — the Spirit overhead will look humorously
malign and cast an oblique light on them, followed
by volleys of silvery laughter. That is the Comic
Spirit." The Comic Spirit is the just common sense,
the subconscious wisdom of the ages. There *is* a

golden mean, the Comic Spirit shows it to us in the light of our flashing laughter at the deviation therefrom. And because there is, even the unreconciled — if reconcilable — difference or conflict is not serious. That is why true Comedy seems to find its best field in a developed social life. The incongruities of human nature hurt if they are pressed too deep, because they are irreconcilable ; they too quickly edge the tragic gulf. But the incongruities of the conventional life do not hurt when pressed. To change our metaphor, adjustment to the middle way is here so easily credible and possible, that it is the very hunting-ground for the Comic Spirit.

The reputed masterpiece of Molière shows us Alceste and Célimène in the end still at odds. But light-heartedness and sincerity are not to common sense incompatible, and thus we are rightly led up to the *impasse* by paths of laughter. Wherever the middle way is divined, there is the possible entrance of the Spirit of Comedy. It is certainly a detriment to the purely tragic effect of Pinero's greatest play, that the middle way, the possibility of reconciliation, is shadowed forth in the last word, — the cry of the stepdaughter of the Second Mrs. Tanqueray, " If I had only been more merciful ! " Dumas *fils* would never have allowed that. He would have written his play around that thought, and made it indeed a reconciling drama — or he would have suppressed the cry. The end of Romeo and Juliet — dare I confess it ? — has always hovered for me close to that border which is not sublime. For the hapless lovers missed all for want of a little common sense. There was naught inevitable in their plight. I see the Comic Spirit leaning across to stay the hand of the impetuous Romeo. Why not take a moment's sober thought? she murmurs.

Tragedy ensues when there is no way out. It is not that ruin or death for those in whom these forces are embodied is of the essence of the situation; only that in the complete destruction of a force or purpose when it has been embodied in a strong desperate character, the death of that character is usually involved. There is no solution but to cut the knot. The tragic has been defined as " that quality of experience whereby, in and through some serious collision, followed by fatal catastrophe or inner ruin, something valuable in personality becomes manifest, either as sublime or admirable in the hero, or as triumph of an idea." But "Lear," "Macbeth," "Hamlet," "Œdipus King," "Othello," exist to contravene this view. No, the tragic (in its first sense, in the sense derived from the dramatic form from which it is named) is in the collision itself; it is the profound and, to our vision, the irreconcilable antagonism of different elements in life. And in life we accept it because we must; we transcend it because, as moral beings, we may. The sublime in actual tragic experience is the reaction of the unconquerable Soul. In tragic literature another element appears. We are helped in transcending the essential contradictions of life presented to us, because the conditions of literature in " preparing " an event create for us the illusion of volition, the acceptance of fate. And in the tragic drama, to all these elements of the complex experience, there is added the exaltation of the æsthetic " arrest," the tension of confrontations.

The question of the " highest " or " most tragic " form of tragedy seems to have been settled by general agreement. It has been held that the tragic of the justified opposing force is the more full of meaning and importance, for the reason that more interesting and complex feelings are called into play on each side than in the case of the un-justified opposing force. But the definition of the tragic drama we have won seems further to illuminate our undoubted preference for this type. We demand æsthetically all that will make the confrontation, the dramatic tension, more clearly felt; and we cannot realize fully a side which should be unjustified. In such a play as Maeterlinck's " Agla-vaine and Selysette " there is no movement, and even the conflict is subterranean; yet, as all the characters are in their way noble, and in their way justified, we find it among the most poignant of his plays. Nay, more, in any situation the more nearly the conflict is shown to be absolutely inevi-table, arising out of the very nature of life as we know it, — completely justified, or at least *felt* as inevitable on both sides, — the more are we shaken by the distinctive tragic emotion. The conflict of duties to one's self and to the world is the sharpest of tragedies. Luther, as Freytag well shows, is a really tragic figure from the moment when we conceive of the inner connection of his intolerance with all that is good and great in his nature. As the expression of such a conflict of impulses good in themselves, " Magda " is a greater tragedy than the " Joy of Living ; " " Ghosts " than " Hedda Gabler ; " the story of " Francesca da Rimini " (I do not mean D'Annunzio's play) than " La Citta Morta."

What, then, shall be said of the so-called tragic " Guilt," in which the hero rushes on impiously to his doom? It is clear that this question is closely related to the much-debated " Greatness " of the tragic hero. If there is guilt, there must be also greatness, to impress that side of the canvas on our vision. It is, indeed, almost a quantitative problem. Strength, energy, depth of passion, breadth of vision, power and place, ravish our attention and our unconscious imitation. What is lacking in extensity of associative reproduction must be added in intensity. And, in fact, we find that it is the giants who bear the tragic " Schuld." Hamlet is not guilty; rather " one like ourselves," in Aristotle's phrase, and therefore he need not be great. I agree with Volkelt's view that even the traditional tremendous will of the tragic hero may be dispensed with. No doubt it is most often strength of will which brings out the original conflict. But that conflict once given, as it is given, for example, in "Hamlet," the main point is to increase the weight of each side, which can indeed be done by other elements of greatness. On the other hand, I disagree with Volkelt's reason for thus exempting will, which is, that the contrast feeling of "how great a fall was there" may be given by other qualities in the hero than that of will. As I have urged, it is not the catastrophe which is of the tragic essence, and therefore not for the sake of the catastrophe that we should marshal our elements. The climax of tragedy and of our feeling is in the deadlock of forces, and whatever is not absolutely essential thereto may be done without.

VII

The phenomenon of our æsthetic reaction on the so-called painful experiences of the drama has then been discussed at length and accounted for. There is an undoubted emotional experience of great intensity; and yet that emotion turns out to be not the emotion *in* the drama, but rather the emotion *from* the drama, — a unique independent emotion of tension, otherwise a form of the characteristic æsthetic emotion with which we have been before engaged. The playwright who scornfully rejects the spectator supposed to be æsthetic, ideally contemplative and emotionally indifferent, is vindicated. There must be a vivid emotional effect, but it is the spectator's very own, and not a copy of the hero's emotion, because it is the product of the essential form of the drama itself, the confrontation of forces.

Secondly, that confrontation of forces has revealed itself as indeed essential. This is not the time-honored view of tragedy as collision, which has been arrived at simply by observing that great tragic dramas are mostly collisions, making the drama a picture thereof, but not explaining why it must be such. I have tried, on the contrary, to show that confrontation is a necessary product of the bare form of dramatic representation, — two people face to face. But if this bare form or scheme of confrontation is understood and interpreted as profoundly as possible, then all the other characteristics of the tragic drama are seen to flow from it; and thus for the first time to be really explained by being accounted for. The tragic drama not only is, but must be, collision, because confrontation, understood as richly as possible, must be collision. It must be "inevitable," and it must have movement, because only so is the confrontation reinforced.

In brief, others have said that the drama, or tragedy, is conflict, the perfect opposition of two forces. We should rather say that the drama is first of all picture, living representation of colloquy; as such, it is balance, confrontation; and confrontation to its ideal degree of intensity is conflict. No drama can dispense with picture; and so no drama is free from the obligation to add unto itself these other qualities also. The acting play is the play of confrontations.

VIII

THE BEAUTY OF IDEAS

VIII

THE BEAUTY OF IDEAS

I

THE Idea of Beauty has been greatly widened since the age of Plato. Then, it was only in order, proportion, unity in variety, that beauty was admitted to consist; to-day we hold that the moderns have caught a profounder beauty, the beauty of meanings, and we make it matter for rejoicing that nothing is too small, too strange, or too ugly to enter, through its power of suggestion, the realm of the æsthetically valuable; and that the definition of beauty should have been extended to include, under the name of Romantic, Symbolic, Expressive, or Ideal Beauty, all of the elements of æsthetic experience, all that emotionally stirs us in representation. But while this view is a natural development, it is not of necessity unassailable; and it is open to question whether the addition of an independent element of expression to the older definition of beauty can be justified by its consequences for art.

Such an inquiry, however, cannot stop with the relation of the deeper meanings of modern art to the conception of beauty. It must go further and find out what elements, the sensuous form or the ideas that are bound up with it, in a work of art, of the classical as well as of the idealistic type, really constitute its æsthetic value. What is it that makes the beauty of the " Venus of Milo "? Is it the pose and the modeling, or the idea of the eternal feminine that it expresses to us ? What is it that makes the beauty of St. Mark's or of Giotto's tower ? the relation of the lines and masses or the sacred significance of the edifice they go to form ? What is it that makes the beauty of the Ninth Symphony ? the perfection of the melodic sequence, or the Hymn of Joy, the message from the Infinite which they are meant to utter ?

The antithesis between these two points of view is, of course, not the same as that other antithesis between " art for art's sake " and art in the light of its moral meanings and effects. What we now call romantic or expressive art can certainly be made the more fruitful in moral suggestions ; but this fact bears not at all on the question of what belongs fundamentally to the nature of beauty. We know, moreover, that on this matter the camps of the formalists and the romanticists are divided. The Greeks, the lovers of formal beauty, were so alive to the moral effects of art that their theories were in danger of being quite overwhelmed by this view. On the other hand, the lovers of ideas in art, the natural enemies, as one would have thought, of art for art's sake, have been most often impatient of any consideration of its moral elements or effects.

This second question, then, of art as pleasure or as moral influence can be once for all excluded from the discussion. So far as yet appears, the issue is between form and expression.

There is, perhaps, some point of common agreement from which to survey and distinguish more exactly these two diverging tendencies. Such a coign of vantage is offered by the nature of the æsthetic attitude, — for since Kant there has been among æstheticians no essential difference of opinion on this point. The æsthetic attitude, all agree, is disinterested. We care for the image or appearance of the object, for the way its form affects us, and not for the actual existence of the object itself. If I delight æsthetically in a cluster of grapes, I do not want to eat them, but only to enjoy their image, and my feeling of pleasure, as æsthetic, would not be changed if before me were only a mirage, an hallucination, or a picture. It is just the pleasure in perception that appeals to me, — therein both schools agree, — and the only matter at issue is the question of what this disinterested pleasure of perception includes. Is that pleasure bound up with the mechanism of perception itself, or does it come from the end of the process and the ease with which it is reached, — from the *idea*, in the contemplation of which we delight?

One school asserts that the real pleasure in perception comes only from form. The given object is beautiful, through its original qualities of line,

color, or sound, which strike the special senses in a
way that is pleasing to them ; and through its combinations of these qualities, which affect the whole
human organism in a directly pleasurable way.
What is outside of the given object of art — is
meant, suggested, or recalled by it — belongs, it is
said, to absolutely unæsthetic processes, as is shown
by the fact that many things, which we are the
first to acknowledge as ugly, are the exciting cause
of great thoughts and delightful associations. The
opposed school maintains that the meanings of
a work of art are all that it exists for. The presentation of an idea, by whatever sensuous means,
so only that they be transparent, and the joy of the
soul in contemplating this idea, must be the object
and the end of art. The later idealists admit value
to the form only in so far as it may express, convey, symbolize, or suggest the content, whether as
pure idea, or as a shadowing forth of the Divine
World-Meaning.

These theories are certainly intelligible ; but the
results of applying them with logical consistency
are rather terrifying. Andrew Lang says somewhere that the logical consequence of the formal
theory of art in all its nakedness would make
Tennyson the youth, Swinburne, and Edgar Poe
the greatest poets of the world, and those delicious
effusions of Edward Lear, " The Jumblies " and
" On the Coast of Coromandel," masterpieces. Yet
if we allow the idealists to pass sentence, what

shall become of our treasures in "Kubla Khan," or "Ueber allen Gipfeln," or "La Nuit de Décembre"? The results of such a judgment day would be even more appalling to the true lover of poetry. Moreover, if the idea, the end of art, need not reside in the object itself, but may arise therefrom by subtle suggestion, the complications of poetry or painting are unnecessary. A geometric figure may remind us of the constitution of the world of space, a sundial, of the transitoriness of human existence, and with a " chorus-ending from Euripides," the whole sweep of the cosmic meanings is upon us. In the words of Fra Lippo Lippi : —

> "Why, for this,
> What need of art at all ? A skull and bones,
> Two bits of stick nailed crosswise, or what's best,
> A bell to chime the hours with, does as well."

II

In spite of this, however, a place for ideas must clearly be found in our definition of beauty ; and yet it must be so limited and bound to the beautiful form that corollaries such as we have just drawn will be impossible. An interesting attempt to reconcile these two points of view — to establish an organic relation between form and idea — is found in " The Sense of Beauty " by Professor George Santayana. The central point of this writer's theory is his definition of beauty as the objectification of pleasure. Æsthetic experience, he says, is based partly on form, partly on expression, but the pleasure felt is always projected into the object, and is felt as a quality of it. All kinds of external associations may connect themselves with the work of art, but so long as they remain external, and keep, so to speak, their values for themselves, they cannot be said to add beauty to the object. But when they are present only in their effect, — a diffused feeling of pleasure, — that diffused feeling is attributed directly to the object, is felt as if it inheres therein, and so the object becomes more beautiful, for beauty is objectified pleasure. Professor Santayana designates form as beauty in the first term, and expression as beauty in the second term. Beauty in the first term can exist alone,— not so beauty in the second term. It must have a little beauty of the first term to graft itself upon. "A map, for instance, is not usually thought of as an æsthetic object, and yet, let the tints of it be a little subtle, let the lines be a little delicate, and the masses of land and sea somewhat balanced, and we really have a beautiful thing, the charm of which consists almost entirely in its meaning."

Now here, it seems to me, is a weak point in Professor Santayana's armor. If such wonderful elements of beauty can be projected into a fairly colorless object by virtue of its fringe of suggestiveness, why should not beauty of the second term be felt in objects without that little bit of intrinsic

worth of form? Is not such indeed the fact? What
else is the meaning of the story of " Beauty and
the Beast"? The squat and hideous Indian idol, the
scarabæus, the bit of Aztec pottery, become attractive and desired for themselves by virtue of their
halo of pleasure from dim associations. And all
these values are felt as completely *objectified*, and
so fulfill the requirements for " beauty in the second
term." That small amount of intrinsic beauty on
which to graft the beauty of the second term is,
therefore, not a necessary condition, so that we are
left, on Professor Santayana's theory, with the
strange paradox of so-called beautiful objects which
are, nevertheless, confessedly ugly.

What, then, is the flaw in this definition? While
we concede the objectification of pleasure in all these
cases, we cannot, it would seem, admit a corresponding change from non-æsthetic to æsthetic feelings.
The personal attitude towards an object, based on
the sentiments objectified in it, and the æsthetic
attitude are two different things. The truth is, that
all this objectified tone-feeling is directly dependent
on the original real existence of the object that calls
it up, and on our practical personal relation to it,
and is thus, by universal agreement, definitely non-
æsthetic. I enjoy the cast of the great Venus very
nearly as much as the original, — but who cares for
casts of the Aztec gods, or of the prehistoric carv-
ings of the reindeer period? Who wants an imitation scarabæus? To have the real thing, to see it,

to touch it, to know that it has had real experiences that would fill me with wonder and with awe, " to love it for the dangers it has passed," — to feel that I myself am through it actually linked with its mysterious history, — that is the value it has for me ; not a pleasure of perception at all, but a very definite, practical interest in my own personality. If the pleasure lay only in disinterested perception, any representation of the object ought to have the same value.

What, then, the author of " The Sense of Beauty" calls " the beauty of the second term," — the power to suggest feeling through the medium of associated ideas, — we may deny to impart any æsthetic character whatever. Professor Santayana has, indeed, mediated between the formalists and the idealists ; but his theory would lead us to attributions of beauty from which common sense revolts ; and we have seen the secret of its deficiency to lie in the confusion of the personal with the æsthetic attitude. If now we amend his definition, " Beauty is objectified pleasure," to " Beauty is objectified æsthetic pleasure," we are advanced no further.

III

The problem stands, then : how to provide for the presence of ideas in the work of art, and the definite emotions aroused by it, either by bringing them somehow into the definition of beauty in itself, or by showing how their presence is related to the full æsthetic experience. But, first of all, we have to ask how the æsthetic pleasure even in formal beauty is constituted, and to what extent expression belongs to the beauty of pure form. Form is impressive, or directly beautiful, through its harmony with the conditions offered by our senses, primarily of sight and hearing, and through the harmony of its combinations of suggestions and impulses with the entire organism. I enjoy a well-composed picture like Titian's "Sacred and Profane Love," because the good composition means such a balanced relation of impulses of attention, of incipient movements, as harmonizes with such an organism as mine, tending to move toward both sides, and yet unified and stable; and because the combination of colors is at once stimulating and soothing to my eyes. So much for *impression*, beauty of the first term. But it is not only that harmonious state of my visual and motor functions that I get out of the form of a picture. No, I have, besides all this pleasure, a real exhilaration or emotion, a definite mood of repose or gayety or triumph, without any fringe of association, which yet certainly contributes to my feeling of the beauty of the experience, and so of the work of art. How did it come out of the form?

Well, this very harmonious excitation of the organism has brought with it just such an organic reverberation as, the current theory of emotion asserts, must be at the bottom of all our emotional states. A certain sequence of nervous shocks and of vasomotor changes, certain stimulations and relations and contractions of the internal organs have been set up as the "diffusive wave" from the sense-stimulations, and a particular emotional tinge is the result. That is a direct impression, but an expression too. Take the same case on a much lower level. A glass of wine makes me cheerful, not because it arouses cheerful ideas directly, but because the organic changes it sets up are such as belong to the *motived* expression of joy, and have the same effect. A deep, slow movement played by an orchestra can affect me in two ways. It may be that I have usually connected that sort of music with religious experiences, and all the profound and inspiring feelings belonging thereto; and so I transfer those feelings to the music and give it those adjectives. Or the slowness of the rhythmic pulse that is set up in me, the largeness, the volume, the depth of sound, all bring about in me the kind of nervous state that belongs to a reposeful and yet deeply moved feeling. The second experience is expression through impression, through the inward changes that the form itself sets up. The first is expression through the medium of something external, — an idea which brings with it a feeling, — something that does not belong to the music itself, but to my own individual experiences.

This distinction between internal and external expressiveness is perfectly clear for music, and also for architecture. In painting, too, it can easily be traced. We know the effect that is produced by broken lines, by upward moving ones, — like the "always aspiring" of the Gothic cathedral. The low-lying, wide expanses of some of the old Dutch landscapists give us repose, not because they remind us of the peaceful happiness of the land, but because we cannot melt ourselves into all those horizontal lines without that restful feeling which accompanies such relaxation; and our emotion is read into the picture as *æsthetic* pleasure, because it came out of the abstract forms, — the *painting* in the picture.

The beauty of form is thus seen to be inseparably allied with a certain degree of emotional expressiveness in a way that does not distract, like the association of ideas, from the pure æsthetic experience. This quality of expressiveness should not, however, become a part of the definition of beauty, so that it should be said that the greater the emotional expressiveness, the more beautiful the object. For if that were true, such music, for instance, as all acknowledge quite mediocre, would be felt as most beautiful by those who find in it a strong and definite emotion; and a Strauss waltz, which makes us more merry than one by Mendelssohn, should be in so far more beautiful. This, of course, we are not ready to concede; and it seems, therefore, most logical to regard the special emotional effects of formal beauty rather as a corollary to, than as a part of, the essential æsthetic mood. But if we give the name emotion to that perfectly vague but unmistakable excitement with which we respond to purely formal beauty, — that indescribable exaltation with which we listen to "absolute" music, — then we must say that that emotion is but another name for æsthetic pleasure. Objectively, we have formal beauty; subjectively, on the physiological side, a harmonious action of the organism, and on the mental side the undefined exaltation which is known as æsthetic pleasure.

IV

Up to this point, however, we have considered only the relation between purely formal beauty and the various shades of emotional response to it; now we may turn to the original question which we set ourselves, how to provide, in our definition of beauty, for the presence of ideas in the work of art. No one will deny that the full æsthetic experience cannot be dismissed with the treatment of formal beauty; and, although Professor Santayana's "beauty in the second term" may be rejected as a purely individual, arbitrary, interested, and hence unæsthetic element, the explicit content of a work of art cannot be ignored. The suggested ideas aroused by an old rose garden may be no addition to its beauty, but the same cannot be said of the great ideas contained directly in Shakespeare's poetry. Yet great ideas alone do not make great art, else we must count Aristotle and Spinoza and Kant great poets too. Must we then be satisfied to rest in the dualism of those who maintain that great creations of art are the expression of great truths under the laws of poetic form? Is the æsthetic expression indeed the recognition of truth plus the feeling of beauty of form, or is it a fusion of these into a third undivided pulse of æsthetic emotion? Is there no way of overcoming, for those arts which do express ideas, this dualism of form and content in our theory of the beautiful?

Let us analyze a little more closely this notion of the content. Music and architecture cannot properly be said to have any content, although they have a meaning according to their uses, like a funeral dirge and a hymn of joy, a prison and a temple. But this meaning is extraneous. It is given by the work itself only in so far as the form induces the emotion which belongs to the idea, — as the dirge, sadness; the temple, awe. The idea of burial or of worship is nowhere to be found in the work of art. In the hierarchy of arts, painting and sculpture show the first trace of a content. This content, however, is at once seen to be susceptible of farther analysis. The " Sistine Madonna " pictures a mother and child worshiped, which may be called the subject, — but this does not exhaust the content. The real meaning of the picture, to which may be given the name of *theme*, is the divine element in maternal love. The subjects of Donatello's " John the Baptist " and " Saint George," of

Michael Angelo's "David" and "Moses," can be described only as men of different types in different attitudes; their themes, however, are moral ideas, expressing the moral significance of each personality. The subject of "The Angelus" is given in its name; its theme is humble piety. From the infinite number of possible examples one more will suffice, — the well-known "War" by Franz Stuck, in the Neue Pinacothek, — the subject a youth, under a lurid sky, trampling under his horse's feet the bodies of the slain. The theme is again a moral idea, — the horrors of war.

If we now ask whether we can attribute beauty to the ideas of painting and sculpture, a negative answer is at once suggested. It is manifestly impossible to establish an order of æsthetic excellence between these subjects. The idea of peasants telling their beads is more beautiful than the idea of a ruthless destroyer only in so far as it is morally higher; and this distinction, therefore, has reference to the theme and not to the subject. How far, however, moral and æsthetic excellence are coincident is a question for which we are not yet ready. At this point we care only to point out that the mere idea of a picture is neither æsthetic nor the reverse.

But, it may be objected, is not our first thought in stopping before a picture like the "War," "What a wonderful idea"? It is the idea and not the form which strikes us, it may be said, even though we may be quite unimpressed by the value of its moral significance. Nevertheless, this view of our own mental processes may be held to be illusory. What really strikes us is the *unity* of the conception. The lurid sky, the dark, livid faces of the dead — the whole color scheme, in short, is so contrived as to impress directly, as previously explained, without the medium of an idea, with that particular tinge of emotional tone which ought to be also the accompaniment of the idea of the horrors of war. The emotion is thus the enveloping unity which binds the subject and theme and the pictorial form together. In this sense, when we say, " What a wonderful idea ! " we really mean, what a wonderful fitness of form to idea, — which is the same as saying, what a wonderful form, or more technically, what a wonderful unity. That part of the effect of beauty in a picture which is due to the idea is thus the fundamental but merely abstract element of unity, contributing to the complex æsthetic state only the simplest condition.

The case of literature presents an entirely new problem, for the material of literature is itself, first of all, idea. Literature deals with words, and words exist only by virtue of their meanings. Even the sound of words is of importance primarily for the additional meanings which it suggests, as the word liquid first means a fluid substance, and then by its sound suggests ease and smoothness, and only last of all is noted as melodious. Thus since meanings, ideas, are the material of literature, we can speak of the beauty of ideas in literature only by an artificial sundering of elements that are properly in fusion. Yet as we may speak of a motive or musical idea and its working out, although strictly the idea involves its own working out, so we may conceive of the central thought of a literary work, and of its development. But the relation here is not of content and form, like the content and form of a picture; rather that of concentrated and diluted form. So, too, as in music, we may distinguish form and structure. Structure is offered to the intellect — it clears and vivifies understanding; it is not felt, it is perceived. Anything which is made up of parts — beginning, middle, and end, climax and resolution — possesses structure. But form in the intimate sense is the intrinsic, inevitable relation of cause and effect; in this sense, it is seen to be truly content also. In literature, as to structure, it is the relation of parts: as to form, it is the succession of events, the movement, combination and resolution of separate ideas and emotions, which give us æsthetic pleasure or the reverse. As action must follow excitement, or despair satiety, so the relation of parts, the order of presentation, must be adapted to mutual reinforcement. Thus the porter's scene in " Macbeth " is related to the neighboring scenes, as De Quincey has shown in his famous essay. And just as in music the feeling of "rightness" ensues when the awaited note slips into place, so the feeling of "rightness" comes when the inevitable consequences follow the premises of a plot.

The particular separate ideas of such a development partake of beauty, then, in so far as they minister to the movement of the whole, just as the separate lines in a swaying, swirling robe of one of Botticelli's women minister to the whole conception. The catastrophe, in other words, must be as inevitably related to the sequence of ideas as the final chords of a symphony to the sequence of notes. The attitude of mind with which we welcome it is the same, whether on the plane of the responses of the psychophysical organism or of the ideal understanding.

V

But before finally relegating the idea to its place in the æsthetic scheme, we must ask whether the specific emotional content can claim independent æsthetic value ; for we can scarcely ignore the fact that almost all naïve response to literature, and indeed to all forms of art, is, or is believed to be, specifically emotional. Maupassant, in his introduction to " Pierre et Jean," distinguishes thus between the demand of the critic — " Make me something fine according to your temperament " — and the cry of the public — " Move me, terrify me, make me weep ! " And yet to the assertion of

common sense that the desire of the naïve enjoyer
of art is definite emotional excitement, we may
venture to oppose a negative. The average person
who weeps at the theatre, or over a novel, would
no doubt repudiate the suggestion that it is not
primarily the emotion of terror, or pity, that he
feels. But a closer interpretation shows that it
is almost impossible to disengage, in such an experience, the particular emotions. What is felt
is rather pleasurable excitement, pleasure raised
to the pitch of exaltation, with a fringe of emotional association. The notion of specific emotions
is illusory in the same sense that our notion of
pleasure from specific emotions in listening to music
is illusory. The ordinary descriptions of music
are all couched in emotional or even ideational
terms, — from the musical adventures of " Charles
Auchester " down, — and yet we know, as Gurney
says, that when, in listening to music, we think
we are yearning after the unutterable, we are
really yearning after the next note ; and when
we think it is the yearning that gives us pleasure, it is really the triumphant acceptance of the
melodic rightness of that next note. So the much-
discussed Katharsis, or emotion of Tragedy, is not
the experience of emotions and pleasure in that
experience, but rather pleasure in the experience
of ideas, tinged with emotion, which belong to
each other with precisely that musical rightness.
Katharsis is indeed not the mark of Tragedy alone,

although in Tragedy it has a very great relative intensity ; it is ultimately only a designation for the specific æsthetic pleasure, to which I can give no better name than the oft-repeated one of triumphant acquiescence in the rightness of relations. We think we feel a situation directly, but what we really feel is pleasure in the rightness of the manner of the event, and in the moment of perfect experience it gives us. Such specific emotion as may be detected in any æsthetic experience is, then, covered by the definition of beauty only in so far as it has become form rather than content, — is valuable only in its relations rather than in itself. The experience of pity or fear, even though generalized, unselfish, etc., — after the various formulas of the expounders of dramatic emotion, — does not impart æsthetic character of itself ; it becomes æsthetic only if it appears at such a point in the tragedy, linked in such a way to the developing plot, that it belongs to the unified and reciprocally harmonious circle of experiences.

VI

But we have up to this time consistently neglected the central idea of the work of art, and its claim to be included in the æsthetic formula. We have defined beauty as that which brings about a state of harmonious completeness, of repose in activity, in the psychophysical and psychological realms.

This harmonious repose can exist only with a disinterested attitude toward the objects which have brought this state about. Whether the Melian Venus or " Hamlet " or " Lohengrin " live, we care not ; only that if they live, it shall be *so*. In this sense, our attitude is interested, our will is active, but only toward the existence of the form. But with the introduction of the central theme, we cease to be disinterested, — our hypothetical is changed to an affirmative. The moral idea we must accept or reject, for it bears a direct relation to our personality. We will, or do not will, that, in the real world in which we ourselves have to live and struggle, certain forces shall be operative, — that there shall be the beauty of health, as in the " Discobolus ; " maternal love which is divine, as in the " Sistine Madonna ; " that war shall be horrible ; that sloth unstriven against shall triumph over love, as in " The Statue and the Bust ; " that defiance of the social organism shall involve self-destruction, as in " Anna Karénina." The person or the combination of events expressing this idea we do not seek in our personal experience, but we do demand for our own a world in which this idea rules. Thus it must be admitted that there is, strictly speaking, at the core of every æsthetic response to a work of art containing an idea, a non-æsthetic element, an element of personal and interested judgment.

On the other hand, this affirmation or acceptance

of a moral idea implies the quietude of the will; just that state of harmony, of repose, which we have found to be the mark of the æsthetic on the lower planes of being. In so far, then, as we accept the moral idea which a work of art presents, in so far that idea has the power of bringing us to the state of harmony, and in so far it is beautiful. And *vice versa*, works of art which leave us in a state of moral rebellion are unbeautiful, not because they are immoral, but because they are disturbing to the moral sense. Literature which ignores the fundamental moral principle of the freedom of the will, like the works of Flaubert, Maupassant, much of Zola, Loti, and Thomas Hardy, fails of beauty, inasmuch as it fails of the perfect reposeful harmony of human nature in its entirety.

Thus a thoroughgoing analysis of the nature of the æsthetic experience in its simplest and most sensuous form has given us a principle, — the principle of unity in harmonious functioning, — which has enabled us to follow the track of beauty into the more complex realms of ideas and of moral attitudes, and to discover that there also the law of internal relation and of fitness for imitative response holds for all embodiments of beauty. That harmonious, imitative response, the psychophysical state known on its feeling side as æsthetic pleasure, we have seen to be, first, a kind of physiological equilibrium, a " coexistence of opposing impulses which heightens the sense of being while it prevents

action," like the impulses to movement corresponding to geometrical symmetry ; secondly, a psychological equilibrium, in which the flow of ideas and impulses is a circle rounding upon itself, all associations, emotions, expectations indissolubly linked with the central thought and leading back only to it, and proceeding in an irrevocable order, which is yet adapted to the possibilities of human experience ; and thirdly, a quietude of the will, in the acceptance of the given moral attitude for the whole scheme of life. Thus is given, in the fusion of these three orders of mental life, the perfect moment of unity and self-completeness.